THE IDIOT BOY WHO FLEW

GRAHAM REID is a freelance journalist living off his wits and his wife.

Born in Scotland and educated in Auckland, New Zealand, Graham has a leisurely-acquired degree that reflects either a broad range of interests or an embarrassing lack of focus. He has papers in Chinese Philosophy, Italian Film and Literature, Botany, Zoology and a whole swag in English and Art History.

His writing has covered the arts, diplomacy and foreign affairs, and travel. As well as having won the Media Peace Award and prizes at the Cathay Pacific Travel Media awards, he is one of New Zealand's best known music journalists. His first travel book *Postcards from Elsewhere* won the 2006 Travcom Whitcoulls Travel Book of the Year award.

By the same author:

Postcards From Elsewhere

Further writing by the author can be found at:

www.elsewhere.co.nz

A regular column by the author can be found at:

www.publicaddress.net/randomplay

GRAHAM REID

The Idiot Boy Who Flew
—And Other Travels in Elsewhere

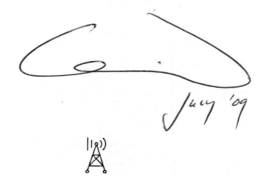

PUBLIC ADDRESS BOOKS

© Graham Reid 2009.

First edition.

Editor: Megan Stünzner.

ISBN 978-0-9864525-0-5

Public Address Books,
New Zealand.

www.publicaddressbooks.com

This book was designed and typeset using
the LaTeX 2_ε document markup language
and the TeX typesetting program operat-
ing on a Linux Ubuntu platform.

Cover photograph © Graham Reid 2008.

Contents

As always, to my sons Julian, AB and Cymon Reid who are out there in the world on their own journeys. Travel safe and long my darlings. As musicians you are doing God's work in this world.

To my wife Megan Stünzner whose love and support and companionship—at home and abroad—has enriched my life immeasurably and sustains me.

And to my parents, Graham Paterson Reid (1913–1986) and Margaret Noble Lamb Reid, nee Stevens (1922–2004). Thank you in your sad absence: you made travel seem part of the contract of living. I miss you more with every whispering day.

A TRUE STORY

When I was about 10 and seated at the family dinner table, my father asked me that most annoying of all questions a parent might ask a child: "What do you want to be when you grow up?"

I am told I answered without hesitation.

"A tourist".

Introduction

�֎

"The world is a book, and those who do not
travel read only a page."—St Augustine

RECENTLY I WAS in a bookshop looking at its extensive travel section: I was disappointed. Not because
the books were dull, quite the opposite in fact. They
seemed heroic and thrilling.

I scanned titles which suggested these courageous
authors had donned shoeboxes and tramped across
the Gobi Desert, had walked barefoot from Caracas
to Cape Horn, or went to somewhere as unfamiliar as
Kryptikistan where they bought a donkey-driven truck
to be dragged through those old Soviet republics in the
worst winter in living memory...

Or they went to Malawi...

I looked at these bent shelves of arduous, and vicar-
ious, journeys and thought these writers were all such
hardy souls and their books were so...

Well in truth, I asked myself: who does such things other than travel writers looking for a marketable story?

I admired the fortitude of these robust adventurers and have sometimes even read of their travels among the ice-cold Inuit, those sand-whipped Arabs, or people who'd just as soon pull out a blowpipe as welcome you into their village.

But that—ice cold and the blowpipe aside—is not what I have done in my recent travels. As with most people, I don't have the time or inclination to do up a broke-axle double-decker bus I bought in Brixton and take off for a year into some snow-driven landscape in search of a story.

My travel is more fundamental, more simple I guess: I go places—and I meet people. Admittedly these are sometimes unusual places and quite often the people are slightly mad, but that is in the nature of travel.

Certainly I have been in dangerous places, have deliberately or unwittingly found myself in some serious scrapes, been where men carry guns or poisonously evil ideologies, and where women are permanently angry and disenfranchised.

And I have undertaken foolhardy journeys into that great wherever that I call "Elsewhere".

I have survived and usually enjoyed the unfamiliar food which famous television chefs make a great fuss about for the amusement of people on the couch at home.

Frankly, it's no big deal. Anyone can eat snake if they are offered some and feel so inclined.

I have been so inclined.

So when I have travelled I have eaten badly and well, sometimes spent hours in conversation with people when we don't have a single word in common, been in odd and unhealthy corners of the planet, and I have slept in rooms I care not to think about anymore.

I don't go looking for these things: they just happen in the course of my travel which is occasionally comfortable but is mostly economic, often tiring and—despite the odds and the unhappily unexpected —always rewarding.

And everywhere—unless the journey proves otherwise because they were hateful, base or corrupt lowlifes—it has always been people, people, people...

That is why the first section of this book—a follow-up to my earlier *Postcards From Elsewhere*—opens with Encounters in Elsewhere. These are pieces about people I have met, almost always by accident.

In that section you may read of certifiably crazy men, poor people, some wealthy beyond our imagining, and of ordinary folk for whom every day is just another footstep on a journey to the inevitable.

Everything is the truth as I have seen it, but as I mentioned in my introduction to *Postcards from Elsewhere*, the Rastafarians have a saying I respect: No truth, only versions.

They are the Encounters in Elsewhere which open this unashamedly free-wheeling collection.

As with many who travel, I have also been fortunate to find myself in unexpected places which have unusual histories or strange stories attached to them:

a museum in a nowhere and expansive landscape in America's Pacific Northwest which was stacked with Rodin sculpture and exotic chess sets; odd little round houses in a small and seldom-visited part of Italy; the self-indulgent retreat of exotically Islamic art near hedonistic Honolulu; the antebellum home of an American country singer which is gaudy yet fascinating for what it says about that world of earthy honesty and downhome wealth; a luxurious hotel in a 16th century monastic retreat in Italy...

Sometimes sublime food and wine are tangentially the subject; in others it may be disconcerting low-rent bars for the homeless and the hurting; in another it may be unnerving people; or simply me stumbling into a place which seemed dislocated from its surroundings.

These places make for the Unexpected in Elsewhere section.

The curiously novelistic title given to this collection however—*The Idiot Boy Who Flew* —is taken from the final, longer story, one which weaves through time and place, and is my search for an Italian saint I had briefly read about.

My chance encounter of his long-forgotten name in a distressingly cheap, mouldy and unprepossessing book became my guide into...

In truth, I didn't know what. It was an adventure— but involved a decent rental car and not an old bus I had done up myself.

A few of these writings have been published previously, others are my original longer versions now freed of the constraints of space which magazines and newspapers impose. The majority arrive here for the first time.

As with *Postcards From Elsewhere*, the many and varied writing styles will doubtless confuse and irritate as many readers as they may amuse and please.

So be it.

I have ordered the collection so that, despite the heroically geographic leaps and sometimes sideways slips through time, the pieces lead into each other through similarity, or bump up against what follows by uncomfortable counterpoint.

For me that makes sense: that is what travel is about. Our past and the present, the familiar and frighteningly unusual can all collide in that moment when you are There. Wherever that There might be.

I believe we carry with us, wherever we go, some collective memory of our various pasts: those cheap songs we heard in childhood or the lost teenage years which now have some crazily dislocated resonance; the glimpse of a stranger's face at a marketplace who reminds us of a lover long gone; something as simple as the compellingly foul shit-whiff of an alley in a country left behind a week, a month or possibly a decade ago.

Or the sheer joy in that moment when you know you are There, whoever You might be at that moment.

Travel is complex, irritating, uncomfortable, shot through with the unexpected and the rare, and only ever makes sense because the common thread—the only singular thing in all of these fragments of our lives—is that fickle and foolhardy You.

In this book I hope sometimes you can see me as

that You.

So for me to impose some over-arching concept on such diverse content, dissimilar people and different places, and writing styles which are determined by the subject and the unexpected encounters would be...

Well, it would be artificial, like so many of those books on the shelves I mentioned at the outset.

These stories are what happened to me. They could just as easily have happened to you. And I hope one day something similarly interesting does. Not the ones which involve guns and bad places though.

Needless to say, for not one of these stories or encounters did I pull on shoeboxes or walk great distances. I didn't buy a horse.

I ate one though. That is here too.

Auckland, Summer 2008
www.elsewhere.co.nz

PART I

Encounters in Elsewhere: People

Night of the Hunters

(Oregon, USA)

SONNY—THAT'S WHAT the big bellowing men called him—runs a restaurant in Klamath Falls, a town in central Oregon halfway between San Francisco and Portland. His place, the Dynasty, boasts "authentic Chinese food". Sonny is from Taiwan.

This town was originally called Linkville, but a century or so ago the locals decided they wanted a more dramatic name for their home on the edge of the Upper Klamath Lake. So they named it after the waterfall nearby.

Regrettably, damming and changes of water courses means that today there are no falls in Klamath Falls, dramatic or otherwise.

The town is within an easy drive of picturesque Crater Lake National Park so the small airport is busy bringing in tourists and trampers, and Sonny's place on the southern entry does a good trade with people coming up from California. Klamath Falls is just across the state line.

The petite and nervous woman from India in the motel near Sonny's recommended his place to me when I asked if there was somewhere nearby I could have a drink and quietly read the local papers.

And that's what I was doing at Sonny's when the Big Bellowing Men arrived.

"Lotsa shrimp, big jumbo prawns and not too hot," one demanded with a rafter-shaking boom as he took his place in the bar, a room beside the family-style restaurant.

"No, no. Hot, but not hot-hot," says Sonny taking their orders then racing off to the kitchen.

The Big Bellowing Men settle in ordering beers and shooters as Sonny brings plates of steaming food then waits patiently behind the bar as they eat, yell into cellphones and bellow at each other.

"Man, she likes you and she ain't nast-ee. Marty knows some nast-ee women, but she ain't one."

Sonny stands behind his bar waiting, listening to all this.

"I can't remember what I said to her, but she liked my package."

The Big Bellowing Men laugh and Sonny waits quietly.

"Hey, where'd he go? He go outside for a smoke?"

Sonny stands and waits.

"So he says this at my Mom's birthday. You think I'm gonna put up with that shit from him? He may be family but I'm takin' him down, man."

Sonny waits.

This goes on for half an hour, Sonny sometimes jumping to get more beers or fill another shot glass. I sit further down the bar reading about what a volatile little town this used to be a century and a half ago. Local history records that fistfights were as much part of the entertainment as theatres, saloons and brothels.

"And you know what," one of them bellows at Sonny, "why don't you get me a barbecue pork pack with hot mustard and some fries to go?"

Sonny runs off to the kitchen again.

In a rare silence I am spotted and invited with a wave to sit with the Big Bellowing Men. We chat as they pack away dozens of prawns, plates of sliced beef and mushrooms, and fish pieces with fried rice.

I ask one of the guys with arms like torpedos what they are doing in town.

The reason for their appetites and high spirits is because they've been invited down by some local farmers to shoot on their spreads. They'll shoot tomorrow, party tomorrow night, then drive back home to Portland on Sunday.

Torpedo Man in a plaid shirt and flak jacket has a handshake that can crush iron, and another of the Big Bellowing Men can barely hear and has to cup his hand over one ear. He did two tours of duty in Vietnam based in Danang. I have been there so we have a bit to talk about.

Another guy, Deaf-Vet's brother as it turns out, tells me his son is just back from Iraq but has signed on for another tour.

We all go quiet for a bit to consider that.

One of the other guys—big, but a Non-Bellowing Man—just sits silent, looking into his stir-fry and coffee cup.

"He's all right," whispers Torpedo Man. "But don't give him no trouble."

I deliberately avoid eye contact so as not to give him no trouble. Later, when I offer to pay for the coffees we've ordered from an increasingly nervous Sonny, the Silent One looks at me, says nothing for a while, then mutters, "I think I'll pay for my own. If it's all right with you."

The way he measures out his words with what seems like calculated menace suggests it might be unwise to take this personally.

But Torpedo Man is in a chatty, beer-filled mood and tells me he works in a factory on the Columbia River. I guess it to be one of those hellfire places belching fumes I have seen a few days before. We talk about politics for a bit—I second-guess their view on Iraq—and about how dramatic the landscape is around here.

A table of slight and obviously uncomfortable Indian men having dinner in the corner—they are staying at my motel, relatives of the owners—have tolerated the noise for long enough and leave like whispers of smoke, hoping not to draw attention to themselves.

A guy built like an oak comes in with his wife and takes a seat further down the bar.

Sonny serves them. Then he serves the Big Bellowing Men again, then me. Perspiration is visible on his brow and upper lip.

I go to the panelled bathroom and when I come back shouting has started.

Oakman has taken offence at a look from one of the Big Bellowing Men. He is on his feet, fists clenched, chest like a truck. His wife is hitting him on the back to stop him but his anger and horny hide make him oblivious to her.

Sonny, the top of his head barely reaching Oakman's chest, is standing between him and the Big Bellowing Men trying to restrain him. Oakman shouts curses and threats.

For some reason—the beer with brandy chasers no doubt—I try to interpose my body too. I also think this is an opportune time to ask Sonny which part of Taiwan he is from. The room is swimming with fury and tension, Oakman barely knows Sonny and I are there trying to restrain him. He shouts and curses over our heads.

The Big Bellowing Men don't move from their stools which prevents things from exploding. I fall away. Sonny and Oakman's wife hustle him out the door amidst more curses and threats.

I rejoin the Big Bellowing Men who laugh and resume their drinking.

"Hey Sonny, you should've done your kung-fu on him," says one of the Big Bellowing Men to a sweating Sonny as he lurches back into the bar.

Sonny says tightly that he doesn't know kung-fu and takes his place behind the bar waiting to serve them more drinks, a double-something which we toast with.

But then they are done. They pay and tip heavily.

As they are leaving I ask Torpedo Man about their weekend. I laugh carelessly when he tells me what he has come down country to shoot.

The Big Bellowing Men go threateningly silent.

I had assumed they would be after something they could hunt'n'shoot then sling across the bonnet, something so huge its antlers would drag on the road as they drove down to the local bar and spent the night bragging over beers. A beast worthy of their masculine energy and kill-power.

But no. Torpedo Man patiently explains that in cattle country their prey are pests. I nod knowingly, but can feel the Silent One's eyes boring into me.

I meekly change the subject and say it is a good time to be out of the city and the forecast is for clear skies the next few days. Should be great. Hope you have a good weekend.

The moment passes awkwardly.

But big bellowing men with guns and camouflage jackets? Among them a Vietnam vet, a steel worker, and a menacingly silent man?

I wave them and their take-out in Styrofoam packets goodbye, and wish them luck on the squirrel shoot.

I wait and speak with Sonny briefly about Taiwan where I once spent some time.

He tells me Oakman comes in often.

"He bad trouble all time."

He'd never seen the Big Bellowing Men before.

I leave. The night is crisp, a light rain falls, the sky

is a starless canopy.

I walk around the block to clear my head.

On the way to the motel I see Sonny, standing outside at the back of his "authentic Chinese food" restaurant by the rubbish skips, quietly smoking a cigarette by himself.

He is looking up into the black of another night in Oregon.

Big Marco

(Rome, Italy)

I DON'T KNOW his name, never did, and it isn't important anyway. Let's call him Big Marco because that's who he looked like.

I arrived at Big Marco's small hotel in Rome early one autumn morning, directed there by a sad-eyed gentleman at the hotel bookings booth in the nearby railway station.

I had said all I wanted was a cheap room, with a bathroom if possible, somewhere near the Forum. I didn't care if it was small, I'd hardly be spending much time there. There had been no queue behind me so we had chatted for a bit about what I was doing in Rome and how long I would be in the city. He seemed bemused, if not confused, when I said I was going to go and see the fascist architecture at EUR outside of the city, as well as finding a small museum of musical instruments.

He considered this as he scanned his list of accommodation options, scribbled something on a card and said, "You might enjoy this place" as he handed me an address.

Big Marco's was one floor up and when I turned the corner from the landing with its ornate wrought-iron banisters I was greeted by an extraordinary sight: a small but cheerful office with black and white floor tiles, some attractive if generic "Renaissance" prints on the walls, and lace curtains blowing in the breeze. It was a lovely, cool room—and was almost completely filled by the man who sat behind the desk: Big Marco.

At a guess he might have been 30 but beneath a gently angelic, if somewhat round, face his body ballooned. He had hands the size of letterboxes and his stomach rested on his knees. My guess was he didn't move around much.

He was helpful and spoke a little English in a soft high voice, so I made my booking then headed for my small, clean and thoroughly serviceable room upstairs with a view through lattice ironwork of the laundry terrace.

Late that night I was woken by shouting from below, then a loud crash followed by a disturbing silence.

In the morning I dropped my key at the desk and there was Big Marco, his head turned away from me as if refusing to make eye contact. I thought little of it, said goodbye and left for the day. That night when I collected my key Big Marco was at his desk wearing thick sunglasses.

The following morning a man I took to be his brother Mini Marco—same angelic face but a considerably deflated version—took my key and gave me the directions I needed.

That night Big Marco was back, the impenetrable sunglasses still firmly in place. Through a door off the office I glimpsed Mini Marco in a small kitchen. He appeared to be have a hissing argument with a woman just out of sight. Within the hour the whispers had turned to shouts and the dispute was still going when I returned from dinner around midnight.

The following morning I went down to check out.

Big Marco was at his desk but the sunglasses were removed to reveal a magnificent black eye. I was just thinking Mini Marco could pack a punch when a movement in the corner of my eye startled me. I turned to see an enormous woman in a tent-sized dress with long black hair moving across the room like a battleship.

This seemed to be Mrs Even Bigger Marco, and she was mad as hell about something. Oblivious to my presence she berated a cowering Big Marco, slapped her huge hand on the desk with a thunderclap, and ordered him into the kitchen where it seemed he was going to get a proper telling off.

Big Marco, angelic face crumpling towards tears and embarrassment, hauled his huge frame out of his chair and meekly obeyed.

Mrs Even Bigger Marco then turned to me and, with a smile that would have melted the heart of God, asked if she could help.

I handed in my key, paid my bill, smiled weakly and left. By the front door I could hear Big Marco, and probably Mini Marco, getting it again. Mrs Even Bigger Marco's voice through the lace curtain followed me halfway up the road.

The sad-eyed man at the railway station waved and smiled at me as I waited outside his office reading the train timetable.

He seemed remarkably cheerful, I thought.

The Ghosts of Sacramento

(California, USA)

※

IN THESE FEW hours after dawn there is nothing here but ghosts. As sharp California light cuts across the empty streets of Old Sacramento the homeless who sleep under the nearby flyovers emerge like shuffling phantoms, shaking milkshake containers as they look for handouts.

But there is no one around yet to bum coins off, just other ghosts pushing supermarket trolleys of their belongings, and rummaging through bins for bottles and butts.

Soon shopkeepers will open their chintzy stores for tourists to buy cheap souvenirs, western-style carvings, fridge magnets of cowboys, and bland Mexican food. Later still there will be school groups and traffic, and those jostling toward the candy store which sells flavoured sugar-rushes by the quarter pound.

"Sample all you like," the man behind the counter, whose body shape suggests a lifetime of sedentary sampling, will say.

But that will all come later.

Old Sacramento—a tourist quarter cut off from the suited city by freeways, flyovers and decades of urban development—is a different place in the early morning.

Then you may see Sacramento as it once was, if you can look past the shambling ghosts, and the signs advertising crystals, postcards and fragrant toiletries in floral paper.

Then you may more properly feel the width of the 19th century streets, and judge better how the '49ers, lured by the promise of gold, would have seen it. You may see where this city in the central plateau of California once kissed a welcome to riverboat gamblers, opportunists and the fortune-foolish who arrived along the Sacramento River.

The river flows thick, brown and fast here—big boats often floundered in its coiling eddies and were lost—and the old railhead lies silent in the flat morning light.

This is where the stillness of dawn allows you to hear the voices of ghosts long gone.

Sacramento—the state capital despite the dominance of Los Angeles and nearby San Francisco—is a sometimes shapeless city even though it boasts many attractive tree-lined streets and Victorian homes.

Stand outside the impressive governor's mansion in the suburbs, built in 1877 for a wealthy hardware merchant, and you have to mentally strip away the contemporary clatter which drowns out the old voices, and look beyond the suburban sprawl and the nearby Econo-lodge to get a feel for what a grand three-storey home this must have seemed to those who passed by on horseback or in carriages.

Here—up until the Reagans—was where California's governors lived, rattling around inside the 16 rooms which have hand-crafted bronze door hinges and Italian marble fireplaces.

Sacramento is flat—Californians, like Texans, had land to spare so spread out—and it conspicuously lacks a centre. Faceless office blocks and multinational hotels punctuate the skyline, and around them you could be anywhere in anonymous downtown America.

But at Old Sacramento by the river in the early morning you may, only just, still feel a heart full of history and a city once rich in wild adventure.

The BF Hastings building on the corner of J and 2nd streets today houses the Wells Fargo History Museum, but its story embraces more than just those first tenants back in January 1854. It later became the Californian Supreme Court from where the first coast-to-coast telegraph message was sent. It went to Washington and assured President Abraham Lincoln that California would remain with the Union.

For eight months in 1861 it was also the office for the Pony Express, a name which—like Wells Fargo—evokes the mythology of the West.

The legend of the Pony Express riders—young men who answered an ad which read, "Must be expert riders, willing to risk death daily. Orphans preferred"—is burned in the imagination of anyone old enough to have been thrilled by cowboy serials at Saturday matinees, Hopalong Cassidy, and horsemen on an open plain.

Yet, like the cowboy, the Pony Express looms larger in mythology than it lasted in reality. Eighteen months after it started, the overland telegraph was completed and so the horsemen—who could make an average of 120 kilometres in a nine hour ride—were no longer required.

They too became ghosts, preserved in sepia-toned memory.

Across from the Hastings Building is a statue erected to the memory of the Pony Express riders. It is of a heroic young man on a rearing horse, his mouth agape, determination in his piercing eyes.

Behind him is the cutting edge of a freeway and, on this clear morning, I try to take an emblematic photograph of this monument to a brief, defining period in Sacramento's life 150 years ago. But the freeway is there in every snap of the shutter: the new imposing itself on the old.

Behind me the wooden stores—where once ne'er-do-wells socked back shots of Redeye—are opening to sell trinkets to tourists in trainers. The air is warm but full of the scent of something lost. The outlaws and the West have been tamed, and the old saloons now sell candy by the bucketload.

Then, from out of the shadows behind the statue of the frozen rider, the figure of a powerful man emerges. He is in his late 50s, his thick blonde hair pulled back and hanging in greasy strands to his shoulders, his beard is full and tobacco stained, his pale blue eyes striking.

In a previous lifetime he might have helmed a stagecoach across the dry plains or through the Indian Nation, he might have ridden for the Pony Express when he had been young and daring and fearless.

But he emerges, nameless, from the underpass. He holds an empty milkshake container.

Another morning ghost of Sacramento.

The Rock and a Hard Place

(Guam, Western Pacific)

�֎

Two places I thought I'd never go were Guam, and a Hard Rock Café.

Guam—an island-cum-aircraft carrier for the American military in the western Pacific—always seemed well off any track; and a Hard Rock Café because turning the rock music revolution into marketing with a side order of fries isn't my idea of progress.

The only fast food enterprise I have genuinely enjoyed was the fabulous failure that was the Fashion Café franchise: a restaurant chain based on the reputations of catwalk models, people who famously don't eat.

And as with Planet Hollywoods—where the Hollywood-obsessed brainlessly believe Bruce Willis might drop by for a beef-burger—the whole Hard Rock Café thing just seems calculated and cynical.

I walked through the Hard Rock Café on the Gold
Coast in Australia by pure accident once, but the only
one I have ever eaten in one was, oddly enough, in
Guam.

This tiny island which rises from the sea with all
the exoticism of a billiard table was just a stop-over
on the way to Korea with a group of former soldiers
going back for commemorations of that war which has
become a footnote of the mid 20th century.

I was in Guam, a territory of the United States, for
less than 24 hours but even so some clear impressions
were made. Notably I wouldn't live there if you paid
me—which is what the US military was doing with hundreds of personnel at Andersen Air Force Base which
boasted the somewhat scary motto, "Prepared to Pre-
vail".

We landed at the base but were immediately bussed
out: "No photographs" we were told by a soldier who
was an advertisement for working out, or massive consumption of steroids. Dozen of the old boys snapped
away until their cameras ran dry.

We travelled towards the capital Agana through
tropical streets where the local Chamorro and Fil-
ipino population clearly weren't having life quite so
comfortable—giving the lie to trickledown economics
if nothing else—and ended up in the hotel district
overlooking the photogenic harbour. The hotel had
a high quota of Japanese honeymoon couples, the island's other steady income.

A few of us wandered into the city which lay below,
ambling past shops which sold mostly memorabilia to

the honeymoon couples, and decided to get something to eat. I was keen on the Asian and other cheap places up various alleys but my companions wanted burgers and the like—which the local Hard Rock Café could be relied on to deliver.

The place was almost empty and the music from a lonely DJ quite deafening.

Our honey blonde, cheerleader waitress was the bright spot. She looked like a heavily made up 14-year old—she was 19—and came from somewhere in the Midwest.

Her story was as simple as it was sad to me: she was married and her equally young husband had been posted to Andersen, but she was bored on the base and so had taken a job in town. He really didn't like that.

She was hoping that when they got back to the States she could finish college. He wasn't so happy about that either.

She seemed trapped by her choices, and those imposed on her by her husband's army life.

American military bases are enclaves from which you need never leave: your material wants from Baby Ruth chocolate bars to flat screen televisions are on sale; there are gymnasiums, banks and cinemas; Andersen has two schools; and there is Armed Forces Television which screens sitcoms and so on from home.

The channel also offers public service advice for the young and the fearful in the military, like be cautious—if not downright afraid—of the people in whose country you are a guest.

If you are 19, high on energy but low on life experiences, this kind of message must make you unnaturally suspicious of the people outside the walls of your compound, the people you are ostensibly there to protect.

So I understood her concerns, and could also appreciate—if not agree with—what her young husband must feel about her being Out There in the off-base world.

She brought our burgers—"Here y'are, y'all"—and went back to her station.

Later I looked in her direction, she was standing by the cash register and staring into space.

It is impossible and improper to assume what someone else might be thinking. But I fancied that in those lost moments she was back in the plains of the Midwest, back when her boyfriend was free and full of life, back when she had a future bigger than a burger bar and it stretched before her like the open range.

Back when she had never heard of a remote, flat rock in the western Pacific called Guam.

The Unhappy Isles

(Honiara, Solomon Islands)

�֍

IT IS CALLED the Point Cruz Yacht Club, but the name elevates it. It's just a slightly shabby but enjoyable seafront bar in Honiara, the capital of the strife-riven Solomon Islands. The Club is a haven for expat officials, cash-only businessmen, local doctors and lawyers, politicians and shopkeepers, and rogue traders of this part of the western Pacific who gather daily to drink SolBrew or something stronger and talk over the events of the day.

And Honiara, a rundown town of a few broken streets working on gossip and rumour, is always full of events to discuss.

I was there in the wake of what they euphemistically called the "ethnic tensions", which is a polite way of talking around the massacres that had happened, and the still-simmering tensions between people from the

nearby island of Malaita and those here on Guadal-
canal.

Two days before I arrived in the Solomons the
Prime Minister's special adviser was the target of an
assassination attempt as he left his house. On the final day disgruntled "special constables"—former rebels
who had been given the status of unofficial policemen
in an attempt to placate them—took to the streets for
a noisy and potentially violent parade as they protested
that promised cheques hadn't arrived.

Honiara was volatile but generally safe—there were
no visible guns despite the occasional shots in the
night—although politicians were keeping out of sight
because, as ex pat Kenneth from Australia said one
night over a SolBrew at Point Cruz, "A moving target
is harder to hit".

Most afternoons of my fortnight in sweltering Honiara I would go to the Club, sign in as a tempo-
rary member, and get the gossip. In the absence of
radio and a decent newspaper the coconut telegraph
kept information—admittedly sometimes bent out of
shape—on the move.

It wasn't a particularly attractive place: the view
took in a broken-down Navy vessel some friendly government had bequeathed the Solomons, and of kids div-
ing off the pier. One afternoon while swatting away
malarial mosquitos I noticed a family of rats leave the
club's kitchen and sprint down the muddy open creek
just a couple of metres away from where I was sitting
with Richard.

He seemed barely interested when I pointed them

out.

Richard was originally from Germany but had somehow fetched up in the Solomons well over a decade ago when it was just another peaceful and largely undiscovered part of the western Pacific.

He ran a small store selling dubbed-off cassettes to the local boys—CD technology hadn't really reached the increasingly impoverished Solomons—but business was getting worse. Music ran a very poor second behind food and, since the troubles began, it was costing Richard money just to keep his store open. But what else could he do?

At the end of one long, SolBrew-soaked, afternoon he told me a story I had heard from so many middle-aged men washed up and emotionally adrift in Pacific islands which had once been their paradise.

Richard had married a local woman some years younger than himself and they had a little boy. About 10 years ago he had gone back to Germany to see his family but had felt like a stranger. His friends had moved on in life and he now had nothing in common with them, none of them even knew where the Solomons were.

But now with his business in free-fall and their future increasingly uncertain his wife was saying they should leave and go to Germany, because he had spoken about it so often. He knew they didn't have enough money to get out and start again in Germany, and that she couldn't stand the cold—or the rejection she would inevitably face from his family and friends.

And so Richard was trapped in a place riven by

endemic corruption, simmering violence and spiralling poverty. A place where he no longer even cared about rats running in the creek just a metre or so away from where he would sit most days, staring at his beer in a country once known to the world—and to him—as The Happy Isles.

Clocking Off

(Rarotonga, Cook Islands)

�֎

AT 3.20 IN the afternoon the clock on the bus taking us from the airport to the hotel reads 9.07.

This could be an early and welcome sign that things here in the Cook Islands—as in most such balmy places in the Pacific—run to a different clock. And so it proves a few hours later when I am sitting in the bar at cocktail hour.

The hotel is heavily booked so we have been advised to make a reservation for dinner. Because we are a large and flexible wedding party, I make a booking for 12 people for 7 PM. But already we too are running to "island time", so maybe we'll laze around in the poolside bar chatting for a little longer and turn up some time after that. That'll be okay. It's "island time".

No chance: at 6.30 an abrasively cheery woman from the restaurant comes over and says we have to go through now as she needs our tables for other guests later. I tell her about the 7 PM booking and she says with abrupt but smiling efficiency before she turns on her heel, "Okay, no rush, just go through in the next 10 minutes".

So the much acclaimed lazy "island time" can run fast too?

Indeed, and run weird. It rains for two days straight and in the absence of anything else to do we retreat to our room and the television. The in-house movies are sometimes on fast-forward so Humphrey Bogart and Lauren Bacall jabber away like The Chipmunks and *The Big Sleep* is over in about 20 minutes. Bruce Willis in something we cannot decipher looks like a sprinter on speed, his small sidekick like a mouse on meth.

Meanwhile outside the minutes drag like hours in the traditional "island time" way.

My friend from Avarua, the main town on Rarotonga which is little more than a conglomeration of retail outlets and couple of cafes, says he'll come around 5 PM. He turns up at 7 PM.

A shop sign in the hotel says "Open 9–5". It opens around 11-ish and closes by 4 PM. No one worries, this is "island time".

Only cocktail hour at 5 PM seems fixed and despite the absence of a functioning body clock, now bewildered by swims at dawn and evening walks through tropical gardens, I still manage to make that with diligent efficiency.

The days drift by, punctuated by meals. Time is flexible, two hours can take all day, and the days disappear into one another.

A week later I am in the lobby settling the bill when an Australian approaches the desk. He appears unnaturally tense in this relaxed setting.

He says quietly but forcefully to the woman behind the counter that he really needs to get into the safe in his room. He says pointedly he has been asking for three days for someone to come and prise it open as it seems to be jammed. He says he needs their passports out of it as they leave on Monday.

It is only Saturday, but given no one has done anything about it so far he sees the days slipping away and a problem looming.

The woman says someone will come, and at that moment the security guy who deals with such things emerges lazily from a back office.

The Australian engages him: you'd said you be there yesterday and didn't show up, so when can you come and open my safe?

The guy says he'll be there in 10 minutes.

The Australian holds his ground: but we'll be on the beach in 10 minutes, can you come now?

The guy doesn't answer and the Australian insists.

The guy says he'll come some time this morning.

The harried Australian says, okay I won't go to the beach so you'll come in 10 minutes then?

The guy nods and wanders around the desk and into the lobby. They meet on the pathway, in one direction is the Australian's room.

The Australian is edgy but trying to be calm, he goes for one final confirmation: so are you coming in

10 minutes then?

The security guy says yes sir, he'll be there some time this morning.

The Australian's shoulders sag.

The security guy ambles off in the other direction, the Australian goes to the beach.

Our bus to the airport arrives. It is 12.30.

The clock above the driver reads 9.07.

He Wears My Ring

(Nga Trang, Vietnam)

�֎

WITHIN AN HOUR of meeting Mama Thiu, she was knocking me up for money. Then her brother had a go.

It was at Nga Trang in Vietnam and Mama ran a small, outdoor restaurant at the northern end of the gorgeous beach close to the port. Mama's place was near the centre of town but it wasn't a favoured area with tourists who headed for the quieter sands further down. So Mama struggled, which made her doubly glad to see any tourists who wandered in, tempted by cheap meals and warm beer which could be drunk chilled by the addition of blocks of ice.

For a few days Mama's was my regular because once we got past the initial attempt at a shakedown she relaxed and chatted away about her family, problems with tourists and local officials, and so on. Oh sure, on the second day the motorcycle trip to a nearby waterfall that she was trying to sell me rose in price every few hours as she added in a lunch, then a sister who would come along to massage me.

Mama was an eye-catching woman, maybe in her early 40s, but with rough hands borne of manual labour on the family farm. She had come to Nga Trang about 10 years before and through hard work and bribery had secured herself this small restaurant made of little more than bamboo poles holding up a plastic canopies.

It was monsoon season and at 5 PM the rains would come for at least an hour. It was always best to be in a dry and comfortable place, and that was Mama's with its cuttlefish and squid delicacies, and view of the turquoise ocean and flash lightning over the distant islands.

One day her brother came with some friends and renovated the place. They took down the plastic sheeting then had some breakfast, they took down some bamboo poles and had a beer, then they went off and got more of plastic sheeting and bamboo poles and came back in time for a leisurely lunch. It was slow although not difficult work, but by the end of the day Mama's place was looking, if not brand new, at least much the same as before. But cleaner.

She was very proud of the make-over and asked me if I thought she could now put prices up for the few tourists who happened to come past.

One day the woman who collected the interest on her loans came and for the rest of the day Mama drank rum and became deeply melancholy. As tears turned to anger she told me nearly everything she earned went in repaying loans and interest.

Then she spoke of the French man whom she had met two years before who loved her but had to go back home. He had given her a ring and promised to return. He had written but hadn't come back and she now didn't think he ever would.

The cheerful chancer and hustler I met on the first day had vanished and now there was a fearful, middle-aged and lonely woman sitting next to me.

We closed up her restaurant and I hailed a cyclo to get her home. Through sobs she insisted I have the ring the Frenchman gave her—a modestly engraved silver thing—and that I should come home with her. So I did.

Her place was a tiny room at the southern end of the city, up one flight of steps past bicycles and cardboard boxes of fruit. Her cousin was there watching a martial arts video on an enormous television. The three of us sat and talked, then Mama fell asleep on the couch, and he left.

A short time later I got her to the cot in the corner. She was tearful and apologetic, and insisted I come back to her restaurant the next day. Her sister would give me a free massage she said. I said okay and left, walking to the beach where I sat on the sand for a long time.

I didn't go back to Mama's little restaurant, I think she would have felt uncomfortable. Instead I took the bus to Hoi An.

But I wore that ring for years.

Fire Night

(Golden Triangle, Thailand)

✼

MICHAEL WAS WELSH, a retired fire chief and now he had a great job. He headed his own consultancy and on behalf of insurance companies travelled the world checking out safety practices in fancy hotels and luxury lodges which hosted British tour groups.

As far as I could tell that meant he would make sure the sprinklers and alarms were working, and that the appropriate warning signs were placed prominently around the pool.

Of course he'd stay in these expensive hotels for a day or two as a guest, chat with the manager and inevitably end up in the restaurant or bar. That seemed like a good job, the only downside was that in most places around the world he couldn't indulge in talking about his first love: rugby.

Which is why—when we should have been admiring the view of the infinity pool and jungle outside the window as we sat in a bar in Thailand's Golden Triangle—we ended up speculating on the All Black's World Cup prospects and reminisced about the godlike genius of Barry John.

Our conversation baffled the few Thai and Scandinavians in our company, but we were lost in a world of our own, and Michael had a fund of fascinating rugby anecdotes. I guessed he had been a well-rated referee in Wales at some stage, but now—like me—he was in his 50s and very much the spectator.

Michael was a wonderfully melodic storyteller and recounted a darkly humorous story about an incident when he had been a fireman: the old woman who had died was laid out in the upper floor of a terrace house, a fire broke out in the kitchen below, the brigade arrived and in carrying the coffin downstairs he slipped, the coffin and its contents bounced all the way to the bottom...

The way he told it, full of pauses for effect and wry turns of phrase, had me doubled up with laughter. And then he told another story, and another.

We joked about how lucky we were to be in such mutually fine company, and we wondered openly what we had done to deserve such a fortunate life, me writing travel stories and fetching up here by good fortune, and he traipsing around the world after a lifetime of working for the fire department.

Then as the night went on Michael told other stories: of the apartment fire where he couldn't get through the smoke and heat to rescue the baby; of the young fireman who dived through a window into the unknown on the other side to find a trapped woman; of breaking glass and screaming from within a smoke-filled building; of blackened bodies and crying families...

As we went back to our separate rooms with their petal-filled baths, turn-down service and view across a humid Asian jungle, I knew what Michael had done to deserve the life he was now enjoying.

Home and Away

(Yasawa Islands, Fiji)

✻

BACK HOME IN Buffalo I guess Sue was just another
overweight, middle-aged American woman with bottle-
bottom glasses sitting at a computer. She worked in
her dad's company and admitted the job was pretty
boring, that's why she had to get out.

She and I were lounging in the shallows off a beach
of blotter-paper white sand at Nanuya-Lailai Island,
one of those postcard places in Fiji's Yasawa group
where cruise ships plod around at something slower
than a walking pace.

We were on one such cruise, three yawning days
and four cocktail-filled nights on the exotically-named
Mystique Princess, and now—three days in—I finally
had the chance to talk to Sue.

She had been our mystery woman who hadn't
turned up at life-jacket drill as we pulled out of the

43

port of Lautoka under a menacing blue-black sky.

By dusk the horizon was being cut by jags of lightning, the thick air punctuated by the low rumble of
rolling thunder. It was thrilling and magical as we few
passengers—fewer than a couple of dozen of us, and no
Sue—sat on the quarterdeck nursing fruity cocktails
and chatting.

Talk turned to absent Sue whom we had heard
about already: she had been on 20 previous cruises
apparently—which explained why she could dispense
with the inconvenience of life-jacket drill.

We'd heard she wasn't wealthy, but this was just
how she chose to spend her holidays. We nodded then
gazed across the darkening, inky blue ocean in silence.

It was at the champagne dinner an hour later I saw
her, pointed out to me by a fellow journalist who'd done
some snooping. She was, of course, at the captain's
table.

With one cocktail too many inside him and fired by
the need to know, the journalist lurched off, interrupted
their conversation and asked Sue directly why she kept
coming back.

He returned to our group no wiser and slightly
crestfallen.

She'd laughed and told him, "You'll know by the
third day".

After dinner most of us retired to the quarterdeck
and looked into the endless night again. A couple of
us who had not been on cruises previously wondered
aloud if this was going to be interesting.

For days—between reading, dozing in the sun under palm trees, swimming, visiting local villages, eating, singing after a kava-drinking session, and sleeping dreamlessly—I considered a bigger question: Why do we cruise?

I discreetly asked everyone on board and the answers were various, but illuminating. They reminded me of how we live our lives.

On this trip we cruised to drop out of life for a while and to take back time stolen from us by our daily waking grind.

We cruise to have the comfort and convenience of our own cabin as a retreat, somewhere to settle without constantly packing and unpacking. To enjoy the companionship of others who are also there to relax and are prepared to hold up their end of dinner-table conversation.

We cruise to read trashy books, or start the important novels which have lain unopened on our bedside tables for months. We cruise to escape the children—or parents—for a while, to let go of the small things and remember who we really were before life overtook us. To pull on the handbrake and be where we observe no clocks or deadlines, hear no phones, assume no responsibilities.

We cruise to live by the longer rhythms of the sun and moon.

We cruise to sleep in or go to bed early, and cruise to have this choice. To do nothing if we so desire because have allowed ourselves that for this brief respite from our lives.

To meet different people. To laugh. To sing even,

because we don't usually have the chance in our other
life. To embarrass ourselves and know that no one
cares, they are doing it too. We cruise to become ourselves again.

And in a world which assaults us with neon and
advertising, traffic and television, and the emotional
demands of the difficult business of living, we cruise to
be able stare into an impenetrably black night wrapped
in a warm Pacific breeze as a long overdue reward for
what we endure.

We cruise to escape the mundane, to live for this
brief moment that little bit higher than life.

We cruise to be in a place where we are made to
feel special in a world which is indifferent to us. To
be unguarded and open to possibility, even if just for a
short while.

We cruise because we can.

Sue and I, puddling about in the water on that
crucial third day, now had a chance to talk for the first
time, and I could ask her why she keeps coming back.
But she had been right at the beginning: I already had
my answer.

For Sue, I had observed, there was also something
else.

In the past few days she had been the obvious
favourite of the Fijian crewmen who joked with her,
tickled her with funny stories, and looked after her.

This was indeed her 20th such Fijian cruise—most
of them around the Yasawas—and she was signing on
again for the subsequent one immediately this ended.

Back home she might have been just another anonymous cog in the company wheel but here she was a treasured guest. She was made to feel wanted, and possibly even loved judging by the occasional knowing glance I caught between her and one of the huge, gentle crew. And she needed do nothing but be herself.

As we paddled in the tepid ocean we joked about those terrible package tours of Miami.

"Oh yeah, the ones where people are always getting food poisoning or the vessel catches fire," she laughed. "I've never been on one of them, wouldn't want to. Too many sad old people. You'd always be wondering who was going to have the next heart attack at lunch."

No such dramas in Fiji. Just days of pastel blue skies, afternoon cocktails and this private island. She had long gone past visiting the villages to buy trinkets of shell and coconut, and didn't even snorkel or feed the fish much anymore. She was happy just to be here.

"You know, my friends don't know anything about Fiji," she said. "They think it's somewhere in the Bahamas. I prefer it that way though."

Once, many years ago, she had brought a friend here with her, but she didn't enjoy the lazy days, was looking for something more exciting and less... "less 'native' I think was what she said."

Sue wouldn't have it any other way. The dark handsome men paid attention to her, and here her size wasn't a concern. May have even been an asset in the eyes of the older men.

Everything here suited her. The captain's motto was "the more you eat the better you float", and Sue enjoyed her food.

And of being able to dream, free on the ocean a world away from suburban Buffalo, her dad's business, and her tiny desk with its single glowing eye always staring back at her.

Fortune's Smile

(New York City, USA)

✼

THE STREETS OF MIDTOWN Manhattan were melt-
ing in the late summer heat. I'd already walked three
blocks too far in search of something which obviously
didn't exist: an internet café.

Being used to travelling in Asia where such places
are on every corner I hadn't even considered New York
might not have them in equal abundance. But after
tramping down Sixth Avenue for half a dozen blocks I
was ready to acknowledge the obvious: people in this
city didn't need internet cafes, they all had laptops.

I was frustrated, hot and weary, and in need of
something cool to drink. A Dos Equis sign above a
battered wooden door told me I'd found what I was
looking for. Not an internet café but something better,
an air-conditioned oasis.

49

I pushed the door open and peered into the dark bar and read the place quickly, it was a Hispanic bar and behind the counter was a willowy young woman whose dark eyes and bare midriff conformed to every cliché of sultry Spanish passion.

Three old men in one corner were hunched silently over beers as she rattled off at them. A juke box was playing what I took to be South American folkloric music, lots of quivering and passionate singing over the top of busy acoustic guitars.

I sat on a stool a few seats away from the old men and ordered a beer. When it arrived I asked the young woman where I might find an internet café.

With a shrug of indifference she walked away. I thought that would be the end of the matter and I would have to drink my beer in an uncomfortable silence. She hip-swayed back to the old men and resumed what sounded like a non-stop Hispanic harangue while they listened either engrossed or in a state of fear.

Then amidst the barrage of Spanish I heard the word "internet".

There was some animation from the old boys and in fractured English one of them asked me if I had a telephone line. I said I didn't and they all spoke amongst themselves again.

Over the next 15 minutes things became very confusing: the woman obviously had to explain to the old guys what the internet was—hence the confusion about the telephone line—and then somehow in Spanglish they tried to tell me there was no such thing. Then they argued amongst themselves and with the girl about it.

The situation was absurdly funny so I ordered another beer and sat back to see what might happen next. But it was utterly unexpected.

From the darkness off to my left in the long bar there was a movement in my peripheral vision. A man I hadn't previously noticed approached me and said there were free internets at the public library a few blocks down and across town.

The young woman said I should believe him, he was lucky.

And he was.

This middle-aged Indian man with a slight belly and appalling taste in nylon shirts had won a New York State Lottery. I asked to shake his hand in case the luck would wear off—but then some scepticism kicked in.

But no, he really had won something like $60 million and from his wallet produced a newspaper clipping of him shaking the hand of a middle-aged man in a suit and accepting a cheque.

Of course he hadn't taken the money in a lump sum but had opted for however many millions a year for the rest of his life, and it would roll over to his wife for the rest of her life in the event of his death.

He'd been a jeweller—still was, still went to work—and had been cautious with his winnings: he'd bought a bigger house, given money to his kids for their university education, taken them all back to India to see family, brought his parents over from India and put them in a house near his own...

It seemed the sensible, ordinary stuff—and he still

had the occasional beer in this slightly seedy bar because that's where he was used to coming.

But I had to ask: "Are you still married to the same
woman?"

"Oh yes," he replied with a great guffaw. "I have
to be, it was her who made me buy the ticket. I was
leaving the house and she called me back and made me
take the numbers down and buy the ticket. She tells
me she was really the one who won it."

"And she doesn't let you forget it?"

"Never," he laughed, and we clinked bottles.

I shook his hand one more time for luck, tipped the
young woman, thanked the old men for their help and
opened the door onto the afternoon heat.

For your information, luck in lotteries isn't conta-
gious.

Pride of the South

(New York City, USA)

✖

HE WAS AT the south-west entrance to Central Park on a cool September afternoon, sitting by himself with a bottle wrapped in a brown paper bag.

Pride was his name, "Pride Wilson from Louisiana... but mostly Kentucky". Been in New York "maybe five, maybe seven years".

We walked into the park where yuppies in expensive workout gear would glide by on their in-line skates, and young lovers hand-in-hand crossed to the other side to avoid the slightly staggering Pride and his bottle in a bag.

Pride had been born in rural Louisiana and had such a love of horses he wanted to be a jockey. He'd been a good rider, "but then I grew some." So he worked in stables and became a groomer. He moved to Kentucky for work, had some good jobs.

Then it fell apart. Something about his wife and children and him splitting up, then he'd lost his job because of his drinking.

He decided he'd come to New York where he had some friends. He'd stayed in a brownstone somewhere in Brooklyn with a gay guy who hit on him so he left— "I ain't no gay," he shouted to no one in particular— and then he'd taken to the streets.

We stopped underneath a tree while he adjusted the meagre belongings he carried in small bag tied with a dirt-blackened rope.

He'd got a crack habit and ended up in Bellevue, New York's notorious psychiatric hospital. Then, after he didn't know how long, he'd been released. He'd thought about going back to Louisiana, but he had no money to get there, "and there probably ain't no one there who know me no more, no-how".

He now lived in an abandoned building but didn't like staying there, too many crazy people, and since he'd stopped smoking crack he didn't like to be around "them kinda folk".

So he lived on the streets. He lifted his shirt to show me the purple welt in his side where he had been shot one time. When it got cold he drank Night Train or Thunderbird. They are the cheap wines favoured by those with no money and fewer prospects.

He had some Night Train in the bag, did I want to try some?

I looked at his grubby hands, the filthy bag and waved thanks, but no thanks.

He wasn't offended, but took it out of the bag to

show me anyway.

Just at that moment a cop car carrying two uniformed officers pulled up on the path a few metres away. They had seen an old black bum and a long-haired white guy standing beneath a tree with a bottle. They called Pride over and talked to him in firm but respectful way.

"You know the law, sir. You can't have the bottle out of the bag, sir. So I'm gonna have to ask you to empty it out right here in front of me."

Pride did, then took the empty bottle to the trash-can while the cops watched.

He dropped it in. They drove off.

I thought it was humiliating for him, but no.

"They's jes doin' their job," he said charitably.

We walked back to the street. Dusk was dropping and it was getting cold. He thought he might sleep in the city tonight, he knew a place where a broken window at street level from a factory below blasted out warm air. He'd try to be there early to get a good position. Others knew about it too, there'd be a few of them huddled around for warmth.

We said goodbye and I gave him some money.

"Thank you kindly, sir. You take care o'yo self," he said as he crumpled the note into a pocket.

I guess he spent it on Night Train or Thunderbird, and for a while Pride could disappear once more.

Red Room for a Blue Man

(Taipei, Taiwan)

❈

I wish I could remember the name of the place so I could recommend it—but then again, maybe it's best I can't.

I had spent a tiring week travelling around Taiwan by myself, negotiating train timetables and ticket offices, finding hotels, temples and places to eat—and becoming progressively immune to the charms of dirty hotels, roadside foodstalls and possibly important temples of the kind which had probably ceased to exist on the Mainland.

By the time I got back to Taipei where I could count on a modicum of English being spoken I was weary and just wanted a place to sleep where I could sort myself out before heading to the airport the following morning.

My previous hotel in Taipei had been a rundown, cockroach-ridden place populated by oddball English kids and Americans who were in the country illegally teaching English. It was dirt-cheap—and dirty—but I had no desire to go back there.

I wanted nothing classy like the gilt-filled Ambassador, just a place where I'd be able to get out if the kitchen caught fire, as it looked ready to do in my former fire-trap accommodation.

At the end of Chungshan Rd I looked to my right. Just another block of small street-cafes and restaurants, electronics shops and the local equivalent of the 7-11.

But in the absence of a plan I dragged my suitcase along the rough pavement and at the end of the noisy, motorbike-jammed street I looked up. There, on about the 6th floor of a building opposite, was the welcoming word "Hotel".

I made my way through the fumes and traffic and got into the lift. Six floors up the doors opened to reveal a large and alluring lobby with a marble floor and two women behind a desk who were clearly surprised to see me. I assumed they saw few Europeans. Neither spoke any English.

Through my faltering and embarrassingly minimal Chinese and a series of gestures, miming sleep, a lot of giggling on their part, then some figures scribbled on a piece of paper I got myself a room for the night.

It was more than I had expected to pay, but I didn't have the energy to walk the exhaust-pipe streets again.

The women had obviously enjoyed the transaction

and laughed when they handed me the key.

I was shown to a room near the lift, opened the door, and gazed slack-jawed at what was before me: the walls, carpet and curtains were a vivid blood-red, the fittings and bed were painted gold, and there were mirrors everywhere.

It was an especially garish style of décor I thought, and I started laughing the minute the door closed behind me.

I stopped when I saw the bath which could accommodate three people, comfortably. I ran the taps knowing it could take an hour to fill the damn thing and was trying out the vibrating bed when there was a knock at the door.

A young woman was offering me towels. I accepted them and she stood waiting for a long time. I thought she was waiting for a tip, but then suddenly she spun around and delicately tripped off, giggling as she went.

After my bath I was lying on the bed watching the flickering television and there was another knock. Another woman was standing there smiling. And smiling.

Suddenly one of the older women from the desk called her then came over to bustle her off with what I took to be apologies. It seemed the young woman had come to the wrong room.

I came back after dinner in a restaurant which stank of stale chicken and cooking oil, and the hotel lobby was busy with people coming and going. All night there was the sound of clicking high heels and the heavy tread of shoes outside my door, and the lift doors kept opening and closing.

But I slept well enough and in the morning paid my bill, thanked the older women and made my way down to the street.

It was in the bus on the way to the airport that I did the maths and realised I had got a pretty good deal on the room. I'd had it all night.

Most people only took theirs for an hour.

Into the Valley

(Arizona, USA)

�֎

KAYENTA IS LITTLE more than a wide spot on the highway through north east Arizona. There's not much worth reporting: a chainstore outlet, a small and somewhat pitiful town which shimmers in the dry heat, a few motels and a Holiday Inn.

Kayenta—not far from Four Corners where Utah, Arizona, Colorado and New Mexico meet—offers no reason to stop, unless you are looking for a place to stay before the short drive into nearby Monument Valley where John Ford filmed such classic westerns as *Stagecoach* and *The Searchers* with John Wayne.

So we pull in to the Holiday Inn. This was where Chevy Chase, here to film *National Lampoon's Vacation*, stepped out of his red convertible and made a great LA-style to-do about not signing autographs. When the locals showed no interest in him anyway—

hell, some had lunched with "The Duke" John Wayne when he was here—he sloped off to his room and sulked.

Or so the guy at the desk tells us with great delight.

Monument Valley is cowboy country, the land where iconic figures like Wayne roamed. It is the imagined West, defined through the filter of Hollywood in the 30s and 40s.

In reality Monument Valley is not that at all.

It is Indian land, part of the Navajo Nation, and its history is written on the canyon walls where ancient petroglyphs were carved by unknown hands.

It is easy to romanticise Monument Valley—the photogenic landscape with its distinctive wind-shaped rocks—but that would be to ignore the blunt truth that the Navajo struggle for survival here in thrilling scenery which offers little arable land, and even less in the way of a viable future.

Alcohol is banned on the Navajo Nation but without thinking, while chatting in the Walmart queue one afternoon, I ask a hometown schoolteacher where a good bar might be, somewhere I could sit and chat with locals.

He reminds me of the ban—noting when he lived off the rez he used to have maybe a bottle or two in the house, now he stocks up and has close to two dozen hidden.

But if I want a drink he says I might try Page down the road. Page is at least two hours away. Quite a round trip for a few beers, and which probably explains why the highway between is littered with wrecks and cars overturned in the culverts.

That night at dinner I agree to try the restaurant's non-alcoholic chardonnay. It is so artlessly foul it could drive a man to drink.

Or Page.

We have an early night, tomorrow we are taking on Monument Valley in the company of a Navajo woman we are to meet at first light.

Under bright morning sun Barbara offers a firm handshake. She is a handsome woman with long black hair pulled back from her high forehead, dudded up in well-worn denims and leather boots, and has a smile which reveals broken teeth.

She is Navajo, but one with an unusual history. She has only been back from New York these past couple of years, came home after her marriage broke up, and has brought her two children here so they can all be close to her mother who has cancer.

Her city-raised kids found it hard to adapt, she admits, and while she's had her problems settling in at least she's found a job. She takes people through the Valley, and on this day we are heading away from the self-drive trails and across dry riverbeds into territory which looks desolate and deserted.

For a few hours we bounce across the arid landscape, stopping to admire a towering mesa, an oddly familiar view from a movie, or the traces of former inhabitants.

I have my photo taken at the tree where John Wayne did an advertisement for Aspirin just months before his death. We see where *The Eiger Sanction* was filmed, are touched by the ancient petroglyphs, and beyond a parched creek is a small homestead belonging to a local woman who is renown as a sculptor. And over here is where they shot that sequence from an *Indiana Jones* movie where our hero descends into a pit of snakes.

Monument Valley is a movie buff's mecca. John Ford made Wayne and the towering monoliths, buttes and mesas into stars. Although the broad river Wayne crosses at the end of *The Searchers* is but a dry bed these days.

Sequences for *2001: A Space Odyssey, Easy Rider* and *Back to the Future 3* were filmed around here. Charlton Heston as Moses wandered through this wilderness near the distinctive Mitten Buttes.

But this is also the land where the mysterious Anasazi people walked, long before the Navajo even dreamed.

As others go off to take yet another perfect picture of the landscape with fingers of rock reaching skyward Barbara tells me of problems on the reservation.

Alcohol—despite the ban—is decimating the young and old alike. The Indian has no gene to process alcohol, she says, so they become alcoholics and kill themselves through drink or in driving accidents.

As someone who sees her people with the eyes of an outsider she is also suspicious of the tribal councils which seem to take in plenty of government money or income from tourism, yet somehow it doesn't trickle down to those most in need. The schools are under-resourced, the young people have nothing to do in this remote land, the old people have given up hope.

There is an educated middle generation keen to make progress without sacrificing tradition, but the tribal hierarchy must be respected and so...

Her voice trails off and we stand in silence amidst a landscape best measured in millions of years and Navajo myth.

Barbara is facing the sun which is setting golden-red behind a mesa, her hair blowing back in the breeze. She appears to be looking at something invisible in the distance.

Possibly the past, possibly the future.

Tales from the Riverbank

(California, USA)

�֍

THE FACT WAS, when you walked from the cool, fresh air of the Sacramento River outside into the restaurant at this RV park, you could barely breathe for the smell of cooking oil.

It coated the tongue and hurt the eyes, and penetrated your clothes instantly. You immediately felt like you had spent a day working over a vat of simmering oil.

Emily didn't seem to notice. I guess she was just used to it.

The Grimes Boat Landing near the small town of the same name was just over the levee from Highway 45, a more interesting back road route up central California than the nearby Highway 99 or Interstate 5. Towns here have names like Sycamore, Colusa and Codora.

The sign to the Grimes Boat Landing and RV Park
would be easy to miss as it whizzed past the car window, but we had been in no hurry and spotted it easily.
I pulled off the road, up and over the levee which holds
the Sacramento River floodwaters back from the plains
of walnut farms, and parked in the dusty lot near the
boat landing.

The RV park nearby was full of trailers but there
were few people wandering around in the noonday sun,
just some fishermen hoisting their boats into the river
and readying themselves for sturgeon, striper, salmon,
shad and steelheads. Anything beginning with an 'S'
it seemed.

Fish here were of legendary size and Emily's restaurant had the photo albums to prove it: salmon that
weighed in at 15 kilos; a fish as tall as the small boy
who hauled it in; two grown men struggling to hold up
a sturgeon the length of a plank...

No wonder so many people come here to fish, I said
to Emily as she prepared a hot beef sandwich.

Oh yeah, she said, handing me the pricelist for the
weekly and monthly rates at the RV park.

I looked at it: $210 a month on the riverside; $90
weekly.

Very reasonable, I said.

Oh yeah, she said.

She told me to be sure and check out Colusa where
there was the smallest church in the world. I didn't like
to say I'd heard that before, about a place in Georgia.

I asked for a coffee.

She disappeared out the back to look for some and I

wandered around the large and rustic cabin that served as the restaurant and meeting place. There were fishing photos and trophies everywhere, bits of mechanical machinery rescued from tips and displayed to look like antiques, and a counter above the bait fridge with reels and fishing accessories for sale. The tables were crude but the atmosphere, the stink of oil aside, was welcoming and you could imagine nights where the talk would turn to the big ones which got away.

Emily returned to announce there was only instant.

Fine, I said and wandered back out of the oily room to watch some guys lower their boat into the brown water.

Emily came out with the sandwich. It was terrific, thick and moist, a meal for a man who might want something substantial before a day on the water wrestling with massive fish.

She went back into her kitchen even though there were no other customers.

An old man walked up from the trailer park.

"How are you today?" I asked.

"I'm keeping on," he laughed. "I've been saying that since I turned 97."

"And how old are you now?"

"I'm 98 in three months. I'm keeping on."

He laughed again and shuffled off into Emily's restaurant at the Grimes Boat Landing and RV Park where the solid air would surely have long ago killed a lesser man.

Livin' in America

(Florida, USA)

✖

IN THE FUZZY Polaroid I'm standing next to a short, goofy-looking guy with a curly blond Afro. He's holding a multi-coloured cocktail. I have a parrot on my head.

The photo was taken at a travel industry function in Miami Beach where representatives of various countries, every American state and dozens of major cities, and many small tourist operators, were there to sell their destinations by day—and party by night. Two days into it and I had been handed 120 business cards.

Del—the goofy-looking guy—came from some dude ranch in central California and while he was an enthusiastic promoter of it he was really in Miami to have a good time. He didn't have to stretch himself to achieve it.

Every night squadrons of buses would pull up outside the various hotels we were staying in—more than 5000 delegates, and me who happened to be in town—and then truck us off to a beach or pool party hosted by some rum or vodka company.

Tables sagged at the centre under the weight of the silver buckets full of seafood, and waiters made sure no one was sober half an hour after their arrival.

The Miami manner of mixing rum'n'Coke was appealing. Tall glass, a lot of ice, and as much rum as you could fit in while still leaving space for a splash of Coke.

Inevitably people did silly things: tragically on the first night a guy from New York with three kids dived off the top of a fountain at dawn into a few centimetres of water and killed himself instantly. That delegation went home immediately.

But mostly people just partied and paid for it in hangovers, or through ending up in the wrong bed. Or by being photographed with a parrot on their head.

Del and I had hit it off on the night of the parrot incident—an intimate evening for 6000 guests at Penrods on Ocean Drive where there were four bands (maybe more, it became a blur) and a dozen food tents serving everything from Jamaican barbecue to stir fry. Later however we'd agreed we'd had enough of loud drunken blondes from Texas.

We'd been at a table with some women and one had complained about all the kissing.

The French, she thinks it is, give you a kiss on each cheek but the Latin Americans do three kisses.

Or maybe just two depending on where they are from. And some Hispanics just do that whole "mwa-aa" air-kiss thing, and "My God, you never know how many of those to do".

"The worst are the English though," she says waving her margarita in an accusing manner in my direction. "They don't kiss you at all but just stand there all uptight, shake your hand and say something like, 'Nice to meet you.'

"They are like, sooo boring."

We all laugh until I say for me the real worry has been the Miami clap.

The table goes deafeningly silent, bouffant heads spin to stare at me.

You can get it anywhere I explain. I come from a country where we don't have quite as much clap.

I can feel the chill descending in the humid night air.

But here, I say, you get it when you climb off the tour bus and the hosts welcomes you somewhere, when your driver has finished his little "thank you all so much for travelling with us today" spiel, after speeches. . .

"Everywhere I go it seems I have to clap."

There is relieved laughter and ice rattles in martini glasses. A couple of the blondes are still a bit unsure of me and make to move away. Del and I exchange a loaded glance.

We hop a cab back to his hotel to have a quiet night away from the loud drinking and to see what is in his minibar.

And so we sat and chatted and swapped stories—

and at some point got to talking about guns. Del had one—he pulled it from his briefcase—and told me he'd once shot someone.

Not dead, but enough to bring him down, he laughed.

It seemed that a few years before Del—who looked harmless in a Harpo Marx kind of way—was the proud owner of a particularly expensive car. He was also in possession of a gun and a cocaine habit.

One night while living in LA and wired up, he heard someone in his yard and, fearing his car was being tampered with, got his face out of the white powder, grabbed his gun and ran outside.

Sure enough some kid was going at his car door with a screwdriver. Del yelled, the kid took off. Del gave chase, caught up with the kid and crash-tackled him to the ground. The kid stabbed at him with the screwdriver—which explained the scars on his forearm, and he showed me the wound in his shoulder—and then got up to run off again. Del then fired three shots, one of which hit the kid in the leg and brought him down.

The kid—maybe 16 or 17—wasn't hurt too bad so Del said he just yelled at him some more and told him to go home and never come near his place. Or words to that general effect. The kid didn't.

Nor did the police—which was just as well because he had white powder all over the coffee table. And he was still in his underwear.

He'd left LA shortly afterwards and cleaned himself up at the dude ranch owned by a friend of the family.

He told this in a flat and unadorned manner—

although at the end leaped up and did a little James Brown funky dance and whooped, "livin' in America"—and afterwards I couldn't think of anything to say.

We shook hands and said goodnight, the following day I waved at him across the convention hall, but we didn't catch up again.

Somewhere I've got that photo of our brief encounter and have occasionally shown it to a few friends who always ask—as if me having a parrot on my head is not worthy of comment—"Who's the goofy-looking guy?"

So I tell them.

Life in the Lens

(Singapore)

�֎

AMONG THE TRINKETS and souvenirs at the Chinatown Heritage Centre in Singapore the photograph caught my eye: a lone boatman, standing up in his small craft, is rowing between some other vessels as dawn light catches in the ripples off his oars.

The image, obviously taken many years ago, has a strange golden tone and in the ripples the camera has captured the instant when shadows made patterns like fish and dragons.

I study it for a long time, and then flick through others in this stack of photographs, framed in cardboard and ready for purchase. Another catches my eye, it is a black and white photo of an elegant Chinese woman in traditional costume holding a stringed instrument like a lute.

These are marvellous images—as is the one of a man in a coolie hat pushing a barrow through a downpour—and I say as much to the old man standing beside me.

He agrees enthusiastically and draws my attention back to the one of the lone boatman.

"Think how long he must have waited to get these shapes?" he says. "This man was a great photographer, this photograph has won many prizes."

He turns it over and there on the back is a sheet about the photographer—Yip Cheong-Fun—and how this image, taken in 1955, with the auspicious motifs of fish and dragons, and the quality of the new dawn, suggest good fortune.

It won numerous international awards and the Photographic Society of New York acknowledged Mr Yip as an honorary photographer of the century (seascape specialist).

The old man shows me other images by Mr Yip and talks me through them.

He is bent and educated, speaking excellent English. I ask him if he works for the Heritage Centre. He is slightly evasive and introduces himself as an author, then produces a book of his writings from beneath the counter. It is about the life and work of the photographer whose work we are admiring.

I tell him that I would like to buy copies of the lone boatman and woman musician photographs, and his book about the artist who did them. I mention that I do some writing also. He is excited by this and shakes my hand vigorously.

He insists that he gift me the copy of his book and

he will sign it.

He does so, laboriously: Andrew Yip, M.Ed. Major.

"Yes, I am still a major," he laughs, "but I will retire next year."

Of more interest is his name, it is the same as that of the photographer.

"You have noticed," he laughs. "He was my father."

He tells me how his father was born in Singapore to an immigrant family from China who then moved to Hong Kong when their son was two. Work was hard to find so the boy was sent back to China for a few years and at age six rejoined his family. The boy's father died when he was 10 and his mother brought him back to Chinatown in Singapore.

He came to photography slowly, had hidden his cameras during the Japanese occupation, and only after the war did he seriously take up his craft and then go on to international fame.

I say this is a wonderful if sad story, and with a flourish he pulls out a calligraphy pen and inscribes his book with my name in Chinese.

And so we talk further and he tells me briefly of his own life, this soldier-cum-author whose book is peppered with his poetry. He has an embarrassing collection of university degrees and was educated in Scotland (where he was a psychologist in a clinic), Singapore, and in Pennsylvania. He headed an education programme for officers in the Singaporean armed forces and travelled widely. Now he helped out at the Heritage Centre, selling prints of his father's photographs.

I tell him that he too has had a remarkable life and at some time I would like to tell his story to people in New Zealand.

"Oh no", he says as he hands me the book about his father, who died at 86 in September 1989. "I am not important, but father's life is very much. You must tell people that he still lives.

"See? Here, in his photographs."

Nashville Cats

(Tennessee, USA)

✳

THE CLICHÉ AND JOKE about Nashville—the country music capital of the world—is that every bus driver, real estate agent, waitress and desk clerk is an aspiring songwriter. Spend more than a couple of minutes in their company and they will be pressing their demo tape on you just in case you can be useful to their career.

I'm not sure what Roger thought I could do for him—we were both at a sleazy run-down motel outside of town—but we got talking in the shade of the courtyard near the empty pool which was strewn with rubbish and windblown papers.

He asked where I was from and when I told him a smile passed across his craggy unshaven face. Turned out he'd been down to New Zealand in some touring

band or other many years ago. Was a friend of singer
Steve Earle's too he said, and I was duly impressed.

I don't know if he was down on his luck or maybe
just moving, but his battered Buick station wagon
seemed to be full of his possessions—stereo, guitar
cases, piles of crumpled clothes and tatty but doubtless
important books—and I guessed that by being at this
$30 a night motel he hadn't exactly made a fortune out
of the music business. Roger was trying to work in this
city of broken dreams, but I was just passing through
on my way to Elsewhere.

But he was cheerful enough, recommended a couple
of clubs where he seemed to be on something more than
casual terms with various waitresses, and as we said our
goodbyes he mentioned he had a CD of his music he'd
like to give me. I waited while he rummaged around in
the filthy glove compartment. He couldn't find it but
promised to drop it off at my room later. We said our
goodbyes and shook hands.

I went out on the town and bar-hopped along the
main drag opposite Ernest Tubb's famous music shop.
Some time after midnight I returned to the motel where
a hip-hop party was going on in the next room. Around
5 AM they stopped fighting, throwing chairs and playing deafening rap, and then half an hour later they
started again.

There was no point in staying in bed any longer.
When I opened the door of the unit I found a CD which
hadn't been there when I came in.

Taped to the cover was a note which read: "I left a
better copy of this w/e-mail address @ the front desk

for you if you care to pick it up. May you have a safe journy." It was signed RD.

As I was signing out I mentioned the noise which had kept me awake all night to the manager who promptly refunded $10, then he passed over the CD from Roger.

Experience has taught me that great music comes from the most unexpected sources. Who would have picked Memphis in 1956, Liverpool in '63, or Trenchtown, Jamaica a decade later?

So I put Roger's disc on the dashboard fully intending to give it a fair hearing. After all, you never know.

It was somewhere near Georgia when I put it on and listened, absolutely engrossed by it. It was obviously recorded live in a bar with a gritty band and Roger had courageously fused country-rock and reggae with stories of hard times and wayward women called Wanda. My wife and I listened to a few tracks in silence before turning to each other, both of us thinking exactly the same thing: this is the most godawful music we'd heard in decades.

I found Roger's demo CD at home the other night and played it again just for laughs. I was tempted to stash it away for nostalgia's sake... but I binned it.

The Sleep of the Just

(Kyongju, South Korea)

✳

THE MIDDLE-AGED MAN was upset I had woken
him at the unacceptably early hour of noon. But I
guess that's the kind of inconvenience he has to expect
if he runs a yogwan, one of the cheap travellers inns in
South Korea which are easily identifiable by the sign
which is like a U with three wiggly lines coming out
the top.

I had seen his sign—which represents a bath—as
I wandered the streets of Kyongju, a city of around
300,000 near the east coast.

The man grumbled and blinked into the light, then
led me past his hammock slung across the small kitchen
and down to a tidy room at the back.

By the time I had unpacked a few things for a day
around this historic city he was in a better mood and so
we shared tea on the steps outside and he told me how

to get to the famous 8th century Buddha at Sokkuram Grotto in the mountains which had only been discovered in the early 20th century.

Kyongju—and the nearby Pulguksa temple below the grotto—are in the most pretty and historic part of the country. Kyongju was the capital during the Shilla dynasty until about 1000 years ago and dates back to the century before Christ.

It had been a single photograph seen in a book back home that had made me want to come to this region I knew nothing about: it was of an incomparable painting of a Buddha on a wall at Pulguksa.

At the bus station in Kyongju a young student had pointed out for me the way to Tumuli Park where the Shilla tombs were—silent mounds in manicured gardens with trim walkways snaking between them—and also where I might find a yogwan which was my first priority.

The man at the yogwan, now fortified by his tea, suddenly became very animated and was keen to show me to his brother's shop which sold the best arts and crafts in town apparently, and also to guide me to a fine restaurant which I took to be owned by another family member.

I would get a good bargain in each he said, and wrote something on a card for me to show.

I assured him that after seeing Tumuli Park I would go shopping and eating, and I headed off. He waved me a furious farewell until I rounded the distant corner.

Tumuli Park is a massive walled area containing about two dozen tombs, one of them internally opened in cross-section to reveal display cases of ancient armour and weapons, jewels and pottery, and other material belonging to the 5th century king who is buried here.

The park is restful, but it was the Buddha in the hills that had brought me here so after wandering back through town, a meal in the recommended restaurant (if discount applied I hardly noticed it) and then I went to my yogwan for a long bath and an early night.

The following morning I tip-toed past my sleeping host, caught the bus to Pulguksa and spent a cool autumn morning under bright paper lanterns strung between the multi-coloured temple complex which staggers its way up the hillside on a series of stone terraces cut into the surrounding forest.

Pulguksa, one of the great sights of the world and mostly untrammelled by tourism in any season other than summer, is a place to sit and have your breath taken away by the sheer beauty of the architecture and the Buddhist art: dizzyingly colourful images of the Buddha and various bodhisattvas line the walls; roof beams and arches shimmer with yellows and vivid blues; in the gardens stand huge statues or small piles of stones built by the faithful...

I find the Buddha from the photograph which has drawn me here. Words fail.

Carpentry is art here and buildings are constructed without nails. Massive beams interlock in a dozen places and they support rooms the size of small palaces.

Most of my day is spent in wonder, and then I take the bus up the mountain to Sokkuram Grotto to see the enormous seated Buddha who gazes out to the Eastern Sea in the distance.

The air is chill here and in some places a crisp residue of snow lies in the shadows.

The Buddha, now restored after centuries of neglect and behind glass, breathes a mysterious quiet on this cold day. There is no one else here other than a young monk who smiles briefly then goes off to light incense in a nearby temple.

The silence envelops me.

Everything here takes on a different kind of scale: the Buddha is ancient, the traditions older, the mountains even more so. We are so high that the mountain range between here and the distant sea—only vaguely discernable, perhaps that line of light blue?—seems to fold like so much brown paper sprinkled in autumn greens and golden reds.

I spend the day doing nothing but looking, thinking and sitting.

That afternoon I take the bus back down the mountain, connect to Kyongju and make my way back to my yogwan.

I want to assure my helpful host that tomorrow before I leave for Seoul I will buy some carvings from the shop he has recommended.

But it is now dusk and again he is asleep in his hammock.

Night Train

(Paris to Venice, Europe)

✳

THE NIGHT TRAIN from Paris to Venice was about
to leave when I heard the noise in the corridor outside
my sleeper: loud American voices and the banging of
heavy baggage against the carriage walls.

A woman carrying a small child and a large suitcase
appeared at the door of my compartment. Behind her,
also laden with luggage, was an older woman who was
obviously her mother.

They hauled their heavy cases inside and only then
spotted me sitting in the corner. They were alarmed.
This was a six-bed sleeper and they had assumed, the
younger told me through exasperated and tight lips,
they would have it to themselves.

I explained that I too had a ticket for this compartment. They looked even more aggrieved but came in
anyway and tried to heft their cases onto the rack above

our heads. I stood up and offered to help but they declined. They struggled, succeeded and then slumped onto the bunk opposite.

A minute later the husband appeared at the door. He was a big man dragging two huge suitcases, each the size of a tea-chest. He also had one of those pushchairs the size of VW which, when folded down as it now was, looked like a small motorcycle.

And he had a baby's car seat draped over one shoulder. He looked like a pack-horse in smart-casual daywear.

He manfully dragged his burden into the tiny compartment while his wife explained my presence. He was annoyed. He'd paid for privacy he thought, but I waved my ticket and told him this was how things worked on European trains.

But they would not be defeated by such uncivilised customs. While his wife and mother-in-law with baby in tow went off to find a French porter and ask for new accommodation the big weary man thumped down and we talked.

They came from Pennsylvania and had taken off from New York a few days previous. They had spent two days in Paris. He hadn't enjoyed it.

Their character-filled hotel didn't have a decent lift and they had been on the third floor "which of course isn't, it's the fourth" he said, because in the States the ground floor is considered the first.

He'd had to haul most of their luggage up the stairs because it wouldn't fit in the tiny lift, and he would be having a word to his travel agent at home who had recommended it.

It had been awkward getting around by Metro so they'd had to use taxis everywhere and they were expensive, the Louvre had been too big and too crowded, the food wasn't as good as they had expected—and last night a guy had held him up with a knife and demanded money.

Now they were going to Venice and would hire a car and drive around. That explains the baby's car seat, I said.

Yeah, he'd been told car hire companies in Europe didn't have them.

Then I mentioned they couldn't drive in Venice, it was a city of canals.

Yeah, but he'd seen photos and they also had streets.

I agreed, but asked if he'd seen any cars on them.

I could see this essential information sink in and he looked crestfallen, if not utterly pissed off. Things were unravelling and I felt sorry for him. The holiday had been his wife's idea, he said somewhat bitterly.

Just at that moment she returned and some conversation ensued. The porter had said he would see what he could do.

The big man said he'd go talk to him as well. I said I'd watch their bags but they declined and hauled the whole sorry caravan of cases, car seat, pram and handbags into the corridor and away. They didn't return.

The following morning in Venice I saw them on the platform of Santa Lucia station, their mountain of bags before them.

I went up and said I was pleased things had worked out for them and hoped they would enjoy their time in Venice before going back to Paris.

He grimaced. It had been their first time out of the States he said, and he doubted he'd do it again.

I got the impression his wife and mother-in-law had done the packing.

And how long were they going to be away from home?

"A fortnight all up," he told me.

The Singer not the Song

(Gold Coast, Australia)

※

THE NIGHT WE scattered my mother's ashes on the Broadwater at Surfers Paradise where she had lived, Silvio sang to us.

I recognised him as soon as we entered Fratelli's restaurant, he had sung to me in another place in Surfers a few years back. The story then as I remember it was that it had been one of his son's restaurants and Silvio, a lifelong restaurateur and with an Italian's love of good food and company, had been singing to patrons there for years.

When his sons combined their skills and bought this new and much bigger place—hence Fratelli's—Silvio came along too.

Most nights he is at Fratelli's singing light opera standards and telling his stories.

When he approached our long outdoor table filled with extended family he asked if there was anything he could sing for us. Immediately my sister Barbara said *You Are My Heart's Delight,* an old song my late father had always sung to my mum, usually at the top of voice in a mock-opera manner and often very badly.

It was a song we always associated with good times.

Silvio was astonished, his eyebrows shot up and he said to me, "Franz Lehar," naming the composer. "But you are not old enough to know Lehar."

I was about to point out I wasn't old enough to know Mozart either but that didn't mean I wasn't familiar with his music, but Silvio was so enthusiastic about this choice he jumped right in, in Italian of course.

He sang with great emotion, his right hand quavering near his ear, his left on his heart. He sang a couple of verses and then, when our polite applause had died down launched into a story. One of many at a guess.

Silvio looks to be in his seventies, is slightly stooped but his eyes are bright and his complexion a nugget brown amalgam of Italian-cum-Surfers. He knew this song—written in 1929 for Richard Tauber my research tells me—from when he used to sing on the stage as a young man. We never quite got whether this was in Italy or Adelaide. I heard one, my wife heard another.

Anyway, it was through music—and maybe even this song which seemed to be one of his favourites—that he met his wife Rosa who also worked the tables at popular Fratelli's in Southport.

He had sung on stage and, as a child, Rosa had seen

him and fallen in love. He didn't know this, nor did he
know it when a few years later he sang again and she
was once more a smitten girl in the audience. But by
the third time she was older and had left school, and
met him after the concert.

There had been much indecision and discomfort because her parents weren't sure about him, but the two
agreed to meet again after Mass on Sunday.

He went to Mass and looked and waited, but she
didn't turn up.

He was heart-broken (he said this as if was happening to him at that moment) but then some days later
he saw her.

It turned out that she too had waited for him and
had been disappointed also.

But she had gone to early Mass and he to late.

Ha, he laughed and clapped his hands with delight.
And they have been in love ever since.

He bade us farewell and went off to another table.

It was a good story and he was probably telling
it again within minutes. But a good story, especially
one about the triumph and longevity of love, can bear
repetition.

And Silvio had also sung us a love song with lyrics
which run, "You are my heart's delight and where you
are I long to be, you make my darkness bright. . ." and
so on. Pretty trite probably. But they brought back
wonderful memories.

Of course Silvio, his voice wavering and the pitch
variable, had sung it unforgivably badly.

Ruined it utterly.

The silly old bugger.

Sex and the City

(Vancouver, Canada)

※

THE BAR-CUM-RESTAURANT in Vancouver's trendy
Yaletown district was a sports shirt and sunglasses kind
of place. At the outdoor tables office workers took
off their jackets, and a few groups of tourists carrying shopping bags of their purchases sat down to enjoy
the afternoon sun and the excellent beer.

Both men at the table next to me were in their 30s.
They were well-groomed, neatly dressed, and obviously
worked in the "no jacket required" world.

Their easily audible talk turned immediately to e-
mails, the internet, various incomprehensible systems
management options, and pixels.

The darker of the two was asking the questions:
how to upgrade his photo options, what were manage-
able rates to maximise the quality of the image, how

about this business model, and what do you think of that number of unique users?

The man with the heavy French accent replied with economic and clear answers, asked probing questions, discussed a new way of producing spread sheets and so on.

They talked about architectural drawings, modalities and modems.

It was impressively cutting edge and both looked the part: men who had grown up with the internet and were comfortable with the codes and language.

The waitress returned and asked if they wanted more iced tea. They did and so chatted on about the speed of internet connection in a conversation which, to me as their unintentional audience, sometimes sounded like a mix of Esperanto and an alien algebra peppered with acronyms.

Then, just as I was about to leave, the one asking the questions seemed about to wrap things up. But what he said next made me order another beer and settle in again.

"Okay, that's all good. Now, I gotta ask you," he said, his voice carrying in the still afternoon air.

"What's the best way to catalogue my porn?"

PART II

Unexpected in Elsewhere: Places

Toytown, Italian Style

(Alberobello, Italy)

THIS UNDISTINGUISHED SLICE of autostrada is almost deserted. Just us, and a gun-metal Mercedes—a minute ago but a dot in the rear-view mirror—disappearing into the distance ahead.

We're in no such hurry so pull off to the Adriatic Coast which has been somewhere to our right the past hour as we have driven up this east coast of southern Italy.

The dismal motels and camping grounds are closed, wind-blown rubbish is piled against fence posts and the skeletal, salt-burned bushes. The Adriatic is a forbidding blue-green under slate-grey skies, the empty beach strewn with yellowed cigarette butts is brushed by an easterly flicking up harsh sand.

Summer is ending and although the watery sun is still warm, local people around here are back at work and the tourists have gone home.

Oddly enough, this is a good time to be in southern Italy. You have it for the most part to yourself.

Last night in Lecce, in the heel of Italy's boot, there were only a few longhaul truckers in the low-rent bar-cum-restaurant of our cheap motel with its view of the oil-stained parking lot beyond the rusting corrugated iron roof.

Southern Italy isn't like the postcard world of the north. Up there is the playground of those seeking an Art Experience: Renaissance paintings and frescoes by Big Name Artists, Roman amphitheatres, and swaggering aqueducts.

In comparison, southern Italy can't compete. Villages here can be unglamorous rather than charming, and port cities like sprawling Taranto bristle with bleak industrialism and soul-destroying apartment blocks.

Casual tourism isn't handed out freely here as it is in Florence and Venice. You work for the rewards and, because the few attractions are far-flung, you need a car.

However this visibly poorer part of the country offers less familiar diversions than a famous Leonardo or the Colosseum. Like the pre-Roman town of Lecce with its brain-scrambling, absurdly overwrought 17th and 18th century baroque architecture by Zimbalo and Cino, about whom surprisingly little is known.

Or Castel Del Monte, a massive, octagonal 13th century castle built on a remote plateau near the pretty coastal port of Trani.

This extraordinary and enormous castle was constructed on the order of the emperor Frederick the Second, one of the more noteworthy, if only footnoteworthy, figures in European history and whose life dominated this region of Puglia.

Born in 1194, he inherited the Kingdom of the Two Sicilies from his Norman mother, and the Hohenstaufen claim to the title of Holy Roman Emperor from his German father.

Life should have been easy given those lucky legacies but, left an orphan at age four, he was under the nominal guardianship of Pope Innocent III in Palermo. He grew up surrounded by intrigue, schemers and those who progressively robbed him of his inherited wealth.

At age 20 he began to assert himself and wrote himself into history as a bold adventurer: he conducted the Sixth Crusade and, through a treaty, obtained various holy places for Christendom which others had failed to secure by military means. As the English writer Jasper Moore notes in *The Land of Italy*, Frederick was thrice excommunicated by the Pope during this Crusade, "first for not going, secondly for going, and thirdly for coming back".

Frederick eventually did go to the Germany of his father—but it was enough to convince him Italy was preferable and he decided, for sound military reasons, to make his permanent home in Puglia, and particularly on sites overlooking the plains of Foggia.

Moore lists Frederick's qualities as "adventurer, tyrant, diplomatist, general, polemist, hedonist, scientist and man of letters".

However to those occasionally dubious attributes

Moore might have added "falconer" as that was Frederick's great passion—and that was best undertaken on the high plateau of the Murge. This was where he built the solid and remote Castel del Monte where visitors today echo around inside its cavernous cold spaces.

Not everything in the south is quite so impressive however.

In Matera are the sassi, cave dwellings carved into cliffs, where a peasant culture—with an infant mortality rate of over 50 per cent—lived in abject poverty until only 60 years ago.

Three days ago we peered into rough-hewn holes where people and animals lived in co-dependent misery. It was depressing.

"You like this very much," says an anxious young man in the piazza later, gesturing towards the sorry sassi. We've been watching a crazy guy shout abuse at strangers.

"It is interesting," I say with a courteous evasion.

"I think so. Yes. Very nice."

He walks away and we go back to the car.

Even the grey, endless autostrada will be better than this.

Matera has been an abysmal digression and our real destination is Alberobello, the capital of the Trulli region in the mountains halfway between Lecce and Bari. The town dates back to the 15th century and the centuries-old trulli—quaint round and conical stone houses often painted with Christian or magical symbols—are the chief, in fact the only, attraction.

"There is nothing to do in that place," one of the

truckers in Lecce tells me with shrug of disgust. "You maybe just walk around and take photos."

That's probably true, but trulli—constructed so they could be quickly dismantled when the taxman came demanding payment of the levy imposed on buildings—intrigue me.

They were built without using cement or mortar, just level upon level of flat stones in two parallel layers, one inside the outer. The two thick walls meant these homes and storehouses were cool in the oppressive southern heat and insulated against the winter cold.

Trulli houses are practical and, frankly, adorable. Especially the whitewashed ones which Alberobello—which has Unesco World Heritage status—use as a tourist magnet.

We leave the autostrada and drive to Alberobello through a steadily rising terrain of orderly olive groves and almond trees. The town announces itself with ugly retail outlets and chain stores.

We park in an empty piazza with a spectacular view across an enormous blue-tinged valley, then a typically Italian thing happens. Three immaculately groomed carabinieri set up a roadblock across an access road to the trulli. They then lounge in the sun, affecting disinterest in the few pedestrians who see them then seek another route.

But we amble straight past them. They don't even shift within their pressed uniforms let alone look at us.

Along this road the town—its distinct sides once separated by a river long since gone—opens up before us. To the east is the new part with its ferro-cement buildings, ugly apartments and a few hundred trulli, many still occupied as family homes.

On this side however is an undulating suburb of over 1000 trulli, blazing white under the clear morning sun and painted with their curious symbols. Their pinnacles offer primitive designs—a six-pointed star, a cross atop a globe—and the effect is disconcerting and mystifying.

Some of the symbols—like the cross in a circle with rays radiating outward—blur the line between pagan and Christian. Others refer to Mercury and Saturn. These people hedged their bets.

Photographs from the 1920s show chickens once ran free in these streets and even now some shopkeepers live in their trulli. But you get the impression most of it is a pleasant but beguiling facade.

Today the place has a Toy Town ambience: the tidy trulli are squat and orderly; the spotless streets are narrow; and the planter pots and uncluttered displays of chintzy plaster replicas of trulli have a whiff of Disneyland. It is a town-cum-gift shop. Cuteness is endemic, the effect only spoiled by draping powerlines. But the trulli are kinda cool.

"I could imagine living in one," I say, "if it weren't for the thousands who tramp through here in summer."

On this day however the streets are so silent we unconsciously speak in whispers.

Alberobello, the trulli part anyway, is manicured but still curiously rustic, and the odd symbols add a veneer of ancient mystery to Toy Town.

We amble around for an hour or so, buy almond

liqueurs in trulli-shaped bottles, and then lunch at a cramped trattoria inside one of the adorable little buildings. To leave we have to do the "mi scuzi" thing to a dozen people. There is much standing up and awkward moving of chairs in the tiny space.

"I couldn't imagine living in one," I say once we are outside.

We walk the streets again and take photos, just like the trucker said we would.

In the late afternoon we pass the carabinieri, still lolling lazily, as thick clouds close over this jewel—or more correctly, buffed rhinestone—of the south. The trulli glow romantically beneath the deepening blue-black of the sky.

I point the car towards the desolate coast again, the road rising and falling through rolling hills now whipped by a chill wind. Rain patters heavily on the windscreen.

Then, unexpectedly at a low curve in a featureless road, we come upon dozens of abandoned and crumbling trulli in the darkening groves and valleys around us. They look forlorn and photogenic. But we don't stop.

The on-ramp to the autostrada out of here is just up ahead.

Crystal Persuasion

(California, USA)

✹

THE HYGIENICALLY PRETTY town of Mount Shasta
on the side of the snow-capped peak of the same
name in northern California has more post-hippie
residue—herbal healers, clairvoyants and metaphysical
mentors—than anywhere else on the planet.

And they are the normal ones.

In Mount Shasta, population around 4000, there are
those who believe a mysterious race called Lemurians
live inside the mountain. These mystical beings are,
they say, survivors of the ancient continent of Lemuria
which—stop me if this sounds familiar—was in the area
now covered by the Pacific Ocean.

Just before the cataclysm which wiped out their
landmass some Lemurians migrated to California, Oregon and Washington state. According to local legend
they live inside the mountain—in the 5th dimension,

of course—and are a peace-loving people. Which is just as well because if they had a few beers, got up an ugly mood and took it out on Mount Shasta locals they could wipe out the world's largest deposit of massage therapists and crystal healers.

The Lemurians, and I am not inventing this, were reported to have been seen with reasonable frequency before 1940. They were, as you might expect, tall and they dressed in white robes. According to a 1932 magazine article, they "possess the uncanny secret knowledge of the Tibetan masters and, if they desire, can blend themselves into their surroundings and vanish".

To be honest I don't know how many people in Mount Shasta believe in Lemurians. Or in the Yaktavians who are also said to live inside the mountain and have a mastery over sound and vibration. They possess a huge transparent bell which is invisible until you get with about half a metre of it. True.

But whoever lives in the mountain it seems to be good for tourism to Mount Shasta where bookshops bear names like Golden Bough, Middle Earth and Crystal Wings.

Yes, Mount Shasta is one scary place.

People come here to be healed, to pursue "wellness", or to have sessions with Beth Beurkens, a shaman. Her brochure identifies "the symptoms of soul loss" as feeling disconnected, experiencing numbness, and feeling stuck in a recurring pattern. All malaises the bored middle-class has become good at self-diagnosing.

Beth will track and retrieve your lost soul for you.

For a fee.

If you've got time away from the massage couch or the retreat at Wellspring—where Sharon offers live blood cell analysis and blood crystallisation testing, whatever that might be—you might want to undertake the most common therapy of all: shopping.

Mount Shasta offers plenty of that. Soul Connections, whose "mission is service to each soul walking the spiritual path" will happily sell you healing tools, Tibetan supplies, ethnic musical instruments and that crappy jewellery favoured by those who speak with a kind of urgent intensity.

They also have a Sound Table, "a wooden table with a built-in harp tuned to the sound vibration OM".

Mount Shasta wasn't my kind of place, just being there made me feel uncomfortable. Women without make-up but with glowing complexions smiled at me unnervingly. We had arrived in Stepford and all the wives were modelled on a young and loopy Mia Farrow.

What takes sensible people to Mount Shasta in the exquisitely photogenic Cascade Ranges is the mountain itself. Regardless of who or what may dwell within it, the 4300 metre peak is striking. It was described by the 19th century poet Joaquin Miller as "lonely as God, and white as a winter moon".

It felt like that as we headed for the peak through petals of falling snow. At the limit of our passage, the road blocked by drifts some two metres high, we crunched into a landscape of scattered, skeletal pines and listened to the silence.

Not a Lemurian within earshot.

Later we left the lonely white mountain and drove back to town. We filled up with petrol, and grabbed our version of health foods for the journey north: pre-packaged beef jerky, Cherry Reds and Gatorade. Then we got the hell out of that disturbing, wellness-obsessed little piece of heaven with its crystals and clairvoyants, and sad folks searching for their lost souls.

We headed up Highway 5 to somewhere that sounded more my kind of place: Weed.

The Sultanate of Slow

(Bandar Seri Begawan, Brunei)

�֍

SHORT OF BEING accosted by a wild-eyed mariner,
I can't say I wasn't warned.

"There's a reason why people don't go there,"
barked an e-mail the week before I was due to go: "It's
boring!" Another simply said, "Don't bother".

There sounded little promising about Bandar Seri
Begawan, the capital of Brunei. But I was convinced
I knew better. If others said it was dull I would find
excitement, something undiscovered and illuminating.

Uncovering the hidden Brunei—in truth only Bandar Seri Begawan, known widely as BSB—was my mission and I would return to announce heroically BSB
should be on any traveller's itinerary, which it currently
isn't.

I knew no one who had been there—and others
thought, because it is an oil-rich sultanate and rhymes

with Dubai, that it was in the Middle East. Even my airline ticket from the travel company had "Dubai" on the attached Post-It note.

And a pamphlet I picked up on landing noted Brunei "has often been confused with the other oil-rich Gulf state of Bahrain. It is also sometimes confused with Bhutan in the Himalayas or Burundi and Dar es Salaam in Africa!"

Brunei had an identity problem.

But I had chosen to go to the pocket-sized Brunei—more properly Negara Brunei Darussalam: Brunei, the Abode of Peace—on the north coast of Borneo.

Not that I should have bothered.

As the message said, there's a reason why people don't go there.

According to its own publicity, Brunei is "a kaleidoscope of nature, culture, heritage and contemporary Asia which makes it a compact, safe, healthy and easy-to-explore family destination". It boasts the best roads in Borneo, and car ownership among the highest in the world.

It should be a fascinating place. It is the capital of the most Islamic country in the region where its sultan has an estimated worth of around $55 billion. He once sued his brother Prince Jefri for embezzling about $15 billion, and he owns between 3,000 and 5,000 cars. Not rejects from Rent-A-Wreck I'm guessing.

Even at first blush, however, it was obvious there was little economic trickledown in Brunei (population around 400,000) and that not everyone was wealthy, although my taxi driver wore a visibly expensive watch the size of a saucer and carried a cellphone beamed in from a decade in the future.

When he dropped me in an alleyway opposite my unpromising looking "rest house", the few citizens on the street stopped to stare. It was as if I had stepped into a weird western, a stranger in town.

My ridiculously cheap room was the size of squash court and as scrupulously free of décor, aside from the arrow on the ceiling pointing to Mecca, a Qur'an and prayer mat, and—somewhat cruelly in alcohol-free Brunei—a framed collage of a Cognac bottle and grapes rendered in some kind of shimmering plastic.

The rest house accommodated migrant workers— six Indian men occupied the room next door, some Chinese working girls moved discreetly in and out— but it was comfortable, clean and my room enjoyed an unobstructed view of a stained whitewashed wall, some razor-wire to keep out unwelcome intruders and a mass of rusting pipes.

This was not the gleaming, modern and wealthy sultanate I had anticipated. I must have been thinking of Dubai. Or Bahrain.

Undeterred, I planned a foray into BSB and its advertised delights: the village of Kampong Ayer built on stilts over the river; the famous Omar Ali Saifuddien Mosque in a large artificial lagoon; a glimpse of the Sultan's residence (twice the size of Buckingham Palace they say) from a point up the river...

As it happened my rest house was four minutes walk from the impressive mosque and even fewer from the river with Kampong Ayer on the not-so-distant shore.

I went around the mosque, picked up a water taxi and was sped across to the village where I walked some rickety wooden pathways between the houses, then was raced up-river to glimpse a tiny corner of a gleaming bulbous thing I took to be part of the roof of the palace.

And that was it.

BSB was a city you could see in two hours and be bored with in three.

As chance would have it, it was also Ramadan so by late afternoon the streets, hardly busy anyway, were empty. I took a photo of the laughably quiet "rush hour".

I found myself walking in circles, ambling through clean but largely deserted shopping malls, and finally out of boredom and in the absence of a bar where I could meet people, I went to the movies.

I was the only person in the 500 seat cinema. Either people in Brunei weren't into the B-grade Thai horror film *Train of Death* (subtitled in three languages) or they had something better to do.

I suspect the latter. They needed to eat at the end of a fasting day and were sensibly at home. Where I wished I was.

After widescreen decapitations, angry zombies and a train racing through bucketloads of blood I wandered back to the mosque which by day had shone like a seriously scrubbed Taj Mahal.

At night it was floodlit and looked golden, its reflection mirrored in the still water of its lagoon. It was breathtaking and I took photographs from exactly the same places as I had earlier so I could compare them later. I watched the faithful gather in this remarkable building which gently exhaled harmony.

Then I ambled around, passed all the same places again, stopped for a coffee in a large cafe where I was the sole customer, and tried to amble some more but ran out of ambling places.

I was in my room by 8 PM and went to bed terrified I would go crazy with boredom the following day.

I did. In the morning I found myself taking photographs of the weird patterns of paint on my toilet window.

Later I went by local bus to the Brunei Museum which acclaims the country's oil industry and long history. More compelling was the gallery of Islamic art from the sultan's private collection: silk prayer mats from 19th century Iran; boxes of ivory and colourful silk sashes; 15th century manuscripts and a model of the Dome of the Rock rendered in pearl; beautifully inlaid daggers; manuscripts made mysteriously exotic by my inability to read the Arabic script...

Even a 19th century shoe-shine box took on the resonance of a fine art object.

It almost made my trip to BSB worthwhile—but then I went to the nearby, and equally deserted, Malay Technology Museum which offered replicas of pre-European Malay houses populated by slightly damaged shop mannequins in traditional costume. A sorry affair.

I took the bus back to BSB, walked past the same KFC and Pizza Hut and jewellery shops and went back to the mosque. Because it was there.

I had a shave to fill in time, bought a drink at the open-air market, walked some undistinguished backstreets—and went back around the mosque.

I sat by the river and looked at Kampong Ayer to make sure it was still there.

Sometimes people would ask me where I was from and when I replied brightly, hoping to strike up a conversation, they would nod, their curiosity satisfied, and walk off.

Everything I had heard about BSB was true: there isn't anything to "do"—if you believe "do" means entertainment and amusing diversions.

But there aren't any, and probably won't be.

Yet to expect BSB to be anything other than what it is would be a mistake. It isn't Bahrain, Bhutan, Burundi or Dubai. Or wherever else people think it is.

I considered going to see *Train of Death* again.

On my final day at the bus depot—a block from my rest house, as was everything in BSB it seemed—a notoriously friendly local called Danny showed me laminated write-ups about himself from various international travel magazines. It says something about BSB that a tour guide is of interest and travel writers felt the need to mention him.

I had him steer me toward the fastest bus to the airport.

It went nowhere for an agonising 25 minutes. I stared out the window at the nervous gay-boy I had spoken to the previous day when I came out of *Train of Death*. He was hopefully eyeing up the few male tourists waiting in the depot with their backpacks and girlfriends. I waved to him. He sent back a vacant, wan smile that was ineffably sad.

Finally the bus wheezed onto the now familiar roads of what I was jokingly calling "downtown" and, as a final irony in quiet BSB, we were caught in a series of traffic jams as parents picked up children from schools between the city and the airport. It seemed possible I could miss my escape flight.

I collapsed into my seat on the plane, listened to the prayer before departure (it either did or didn't work, the flight was delayed due to "a technical problem"), and considered my short time in BSB.

Brunei is so small the sultan could probably carpet it and it has no particular tourism industry to speak of—despite being a naturalist's dream with rare orang-utan, snakes and exotic birds and plants. It has a fascinating if bewildering history of colonisation and sultans, and is the efficient face of outward-facing but strict Islam.

It is the only place where a Customs official has asked me on arrival if I was carrying any wine. BSB could drive you to drink—and you couldn't.

But Bandar Seri Begawan—which, amusingly, al-most looks like Bandar Serious Big One—is what it is. Which, especially in Ramadan, isn't much.

Later, in another country and after a large and restorative drink, I sent an e-mail to someone who had warned me off BSB. I wrote, "Why didn't you warn me?" and said I hoped he got the joke.

He e-mailed back, "The joke was always going to be on you."

Maybe. But my brief encounter wasn't entirely wasted. I know few people who can say they have been to Brunei.

But know of absolutely *no one* who has seen *Train of Death.*

Least of all in a private screening.

In the Tower of the Saracens

(Sorrento, Italy)

※

OVER COCKTAILS, LIONELLO—who owns a luxury hotel in Sorrento—insists we go to his friend Gennaro's restaurant.

"He is a master, he has a gift," he says enthusiastically, advising us away from his own dining room which had, the previous night, offered food that redefined the word sublime.

"But is he fat?" I joke. "I don't trust a thin chef."

Lionello laughs: "Oh yes, Gennaro is a big man."

Megan and I are the only two guests in Dr Lionello del Papa's 50-room Grand Hotel Cocumella which occupies a balcony seat in the pretty town of Sorrento across the bay from Naples.

It is late in the season and, although the skies are cloudless and the weather still balmy, most tourists have gone home. The usually crowded streets of

116

Sorrento are comparatively deserted. And we have Cocumella—with its sommelier, two chefs, waiters, and Lionello—all to ourselves.

We walk to our suite down spacious marble halls between gilt-framed mirrors and antique furnishings. The place is as silent as a chapel at midnight and I'm thinking this could the perfect place to settle in and write that long-overdue novel—but images of Jack Nicholson going quietly crazy in *The Shining* keep coming to mind.

We do nothing for days.

Late one afternoon I am relaxing with Lionello on the terrace beside the stylish restaurant.

We have just returned from a stroll down the leafy path to the end of the property— the blue pool on one side shaded by orange trees, an olive grove on the other—where I have audibly gasped at the view across the Bay of Naples from the white walkway along the edge of the cliff.

Before us in the heat-haze distance was Vesuvius and below, maybe 100 metres down a sheer drop, the sea beside the hotel's solarium had been transparent. A couple of people with snorkels paddling around leisurely.

Around us butterflies and bees hovered in the late summer heat.

It had been an exquisite view through the pale blue last rays of the sun and the experience—when added to the luxury of the historic Cocumella —confirmed why this charming place attracts visitors of all persuasions.

Wildman rocker Iggy Pop has stayed here, says Lionello. "He was very quiet, would have one beer and be in bed by 10.30. Robert Plant of Led Zeppelin came and no one knew who he was."

The Duke of Wellington was a guest here even further back.

That is the kind of place Cocumella is, a retreat from the world where you are left to enjoy the luxurious ambience of the rooms and dining areas, the extensive wine cellar and gourmet menu.

The Jesuits who built this place in the 16th century—it was converted to a hotel in 1822—obviously had a sense of humour: the place is named for the nymph Colomelide. However one of their learned number later, perhaps out of sensitivity, insisted the name referred to the terracotta vase used in the region to hold water, a cuccuma.

In fact the stone well used to take water from the underlying cistern, which dates back to the Roman era, remains at the centre of the hotel's cloister.

Nearby is the old private chapel which is today used for concerts.

The hotel is Lionello's happy inheritance. His late father, an architect, redesigned the original hotel more than a decade ago to turn it into something discreetly opulent —it is a member of the Small Luxury Hotels of the World group—where every room is different.

And of course nearby Sorrento, named for the Greek sirens who lured sailors to their deaths, is the city which drew Goethe, Homer, Byron, Keats, Dickens— and these days hundreds of thousands of tourists. It is a five minute walk away.

Cocumella however—with its sun-drenched terrace, elevator down to the sea and tennis courts—is situated well away from the drag strip which is the Corso Italia.

After a day at Pompeii a short train trip away we retreat to our antique-filled room with its balcony and glimpse of the blue Bay of Naples until dinner in the Scintilla Restaurant and its patio view across the small fragrant park.

Dinner arrives: escalope of swordfish in sesame with crushed almonds; whole scampi wrapped in handmade angel hair pasta with small potato wedges in a saffron sauce; half a lobster and porcini mushrooms with more handmade pasta; mushroom-filled ravioli pasta with a delicate herb sauce; lemon sorbet to give us a breather and refresh the palate...

And that is before the main course of pan fried fish with a light crispy coating and steamed vegetables, then the desert of pastries...

Yet the following afternoon Lionello is insisting we go to his friend Gennaro's restaurant? And so that night a taxi takes us on a winding half hour drive through impossibly narrow lanes, over the hill and down to the port village of Vico Equense and Gennaro's on the harbour's edge.

Here in an old Saracen tower is his intimate and exquisite Torre del Saracino Ristorante, where the cellar stocks over 1200 wines.

From Naples south, seafood is the thing to eat: fat octopi, huge prawns, tasty cockles and white, full-bodied fish such as dentix (similar to sea bream) are pulled from the Mediterranean, some more salty than

Southern Hemisphere palates are familiar with.

Gennaro emerges from his kitchen to greet us. Even without the white apron we would have recognised him.

He is portly, beaming and effortlessly amiable. And young.

Gennaro is a member of the Jeunes Restaurateurs d'Europe, an organisation dedicated to bringing young restaurateurs to greater attention. Their motto is "talent and passion", and their website offers travellers a route planner and booking system to allow for a gourmet tour of Europe.

The defining features of these restaurants, we are told by our sommelier Luciano, is they offer fine dining, an extensive wine list to compliment the food, a convivial atmosphere, and chefs who care.

Gennaro cares so much he disappears quickly back into his kitchen, Luciano chooses an introductory local rosé, and within a minute a taster arrives: a coil of raw swordfish in tomato water.

Our waiter has recommended some special dishes from the menu and so we sit back, let Luciano do his work, and savour what comes. It is unexpected.

Thin, ribbon-like lasagne pasta wrapped around squid, red prawns and sea bass; ravioli of swordfish with spring onions, capers and olives served with herbs and lemon; dentix with courgettes; and unusual pasta of different thicknesses from nearby Gragnano in the mountains with a white grouper ragout in a sweet and sour lemon sauce...

Luciano compliments all these with wines which include a soft white from the ancient Greco-Roman city of Paestum further south near Palermo, and an especially full bodied local red to accompany the truffle and porcini salad.

The food is absurdly good and artistically presented, and we are about to admit defeat when dessert arrives: a selection of mini tartlets, chocolate truffles and jelly with thin twigs of bitter dark chocolate and mini meringues. Arranged on a long white platter in a minimalist Japanese design, it is the culmination of a meal which has been of Zen-like simplicity, nuance and subtlety.

We are almost embarrassed by these culinary riches, and the company in the room: other than us the dozen other diners look like ambassadors, retired bankers, the discreetly moneyed.

When we have finished Gennaro invites us to join him outside, and so on a breezy night in the shadow of an ancient tower with the fishing boats bobbing before us we sit, feeling like characters in someone else's dream.

Gennaro is jovial as he sucks down cigarettes, and we ask him about the odd pasta of different thicknesses.

"They are each one handmade by two old ladies in a nearby village, so no two pieces are the same. They only make 10 kilos a day—and they only sell them to friends."

Compliments on the meal seem shallow, no matter how genuine, so I buy him and his sous-chef a bottle of wine of their choosing. He thanks me, and diplomatically picks a New Zealand chardonnay from his cellar.

We soak up the night, a rare one, as Gennaro inhales cigarettes and glasses of wine.

Megan is chilly so he rushes off and finds a bright yellow scarf to wrap around her. She looks like a beautiful beacon in the night.

In the taxi on the way back to Cocumella we are lost for words, and no better the next day when Lionello asks me if we enjoyed our meal at Gennaro's.

The words don't come out right, but I tell him that in all honesty it had been one of the finest—if not the finest—meals I have ever had. It was a concordance of tastes and textures in an atmosphere which was refined but relaxed, historic yet contemporary.

I tell Lionello that it had been prepared by a young and gifted chef—and one whose rotund physique suggested he enjoyed good food.

"No," Lionello laughs. "He loves Pringles, he eats them all the time. That is why he is big like he is. It is the Pringles!"

You Are What You Eat

(California, USA)

THIS IS JUST AN opinion: but nowadays it seems more difficult to find a really bad meal than a good one.

That is unless you are in McCloud, a small town at the base of photogenic Mount Shasta in northern California.

McCloud isn't on too many tourists' agendas—it is well off the highways and seems to be at the end of long dead-end road—and that is probably just as well if the kitchen at the famous Soda Shoppe on Main Street is any measure of the town's culinary prowess.

I have eaten plenty of mediocre meals in my time—haven't we all?—but truly bad meals are so rare as to be memorable. You can dine out, so to speak, on a story about a bad meal, and in my experience very few people want to hear what delights you enjoyed at some expensive haute cuisine restaurant with white table-cloths.

The worst meal I had eaten before my wife and I arrived in quirky McCloud was at a roadside stool'n'spit place in a dark backstreet of Hanoi.

Let it be noted I grew up in Scotland where a steaming ox tongue plonked on the middle of the dinner table was not uncommon. As comedian Billy Connolly once noted, Scottish food is a dare.

Disgusting looking food—let alone things made from organs and offal—rarely trouble me.

So in my travels I have had fried wasps' larvae, a live snake skinned before my eyes and warmed in its own blood, chicken fried steak in Texas (a perfectly good steak fried in thick batter is a crime against the palate) and other such oddball or exotic treats around the planet.

But all of them were at least edible, and in fact somewhat tasty, compared with the offerings that night in a dog-shit alley of Hanoi.

Of the three pots of aromatic gruel I chose the stew made from horse. I'd had had horse before, in France, and it was delicious. But this wasn't horse. At best it might have been nag.

It tasted grey.

In time I forgave the cooks in Hanoi—although later did note that I rarely saw a horse in Vietnam, live or dead—because they may have had limited or inferior ingredients to work with.

I doubt that could be the excuse at McCloud's Soda Shoppe in wealthy California, housed in a historic corner store built in 1895 when this was a once thriving timber town. This was the town's original grocery, which in subsequent decades became a druggist, hardware store and a few other things besides.

Today it is a café-restaurant and the tacky walls are lined with work by local artists who have all painted exactly the same thing. I guess that's what happens when your landscape is dominated by a massive mountain.

The town itself is 1000 metres above sea-level so the air is clear and heady, which might explain some of the eccentric housing in its half-dozen wide but deserted streets.

It seems that in McCloud if you collect empty bottles and jam jars, or oddly shaped boughs of wood (which I imagine is not difficult in a timber town) then you display them prominently along your front porch.

There is a museum for the more valuable and historic stuff, but since the timber business wound down in the mid-80s McCloud—a more romantic variant on the name of its founding figure Alexander McLeod who trapped beaver around here—is now a town which relies on nearby fishing and folks who want to take in a view of the much-painted Mount Shasta.

The weary traveller is therefore warned about stopping for lunch at the Soda Shoppe with its hard chairs, simple tables and astoundingly evil burgers.

The coffee I ordered appeared in an instant—it was instant—then the burgers followed.

Megan ordered hot turkey and I thought beef and cheese sounded good. This is simple fare and difficult to get wrong—you might think.

What arrived for Megan was cold turkey slices placed between slightly warmed buns, mine was much the same although I didn't detect any cheese with the beef. In truth however it was hard to discern anything in the slops which lay before us.

The chief ingredient, added by the ladle-load, was ketchup. It flowed into every crevice of the buns and fillings, and was lapping the edges of the plates. Our meals looked like autopsies in progress.

We would have laughed aloud but we were stunned by the lush red appearance of what was presented to us with something approximating a smile. We thought of sending them back but this was too absurd to be true, and too doused in ketchup to be edible.

We stared at these viscous messes for a while, I poked mine with a knife checking for signs of life then managed to down some of it by washing it away with sour instant coffee from the chipped mug.

But Megan gave up, utterly defeated by its appearance as much as the torture of drinking ketchup with some solid bits. I took a photo of the whole sorry mess and we left.

Uncomplaining, I paid the bill of US$14.50—to be fair that also included the teabag and cup of warm water for Megan—because it was worth it just for the experience.

No, you can't dine out on a story about what a lovely meal you had in a restaurant these days; everybody has nice nights out.

But ketchup burgers at the Soda Shoppe in weird

little McCloud have been good for a few laughs over dinner tables.

As we drove away, up towards that much rendered snow-covered mountain, I said to Megan, "You know, despite it all I'm still hungry.

"I could eat a horse."

Hotel Headhunter

(Sarawak, Malaysia)

IN THESE MINUTES before you realise how foolish you are being, you could imagine yourself as Martin Sheen going up-river to seek out the mad Marlon Brando: the prow of the longboat pushing through muddy water; humid jungle steaming its way down to the riverbanks; bowing branches and vines hanging so low you sometimes have to duck beneath them...

The sudden and unexpected clearings, smoke from unknown fires exhaling through the jungle canopy, and a fleeting glimpse of a wooden hut on stilts. A shadowy figure disappearing between an impenetrable barricade of trees...

This is central Sarawak, some six hours drive on an increasingly deserted ribbon of road from the capital Kuching to the Lemanak River near the border with Indonesian Borneo.

It hasn't been an entirely pleasant trip as my Malay driver Richard—which I take not to be his real name—has performed a highly focused form of toiletry all the way. He has scraped his ears and picked his nose with force and diligence, and then for the last few hours shaved as he drove. This has involved him feeling every pore on his face and, on locating tiny stubbles of hair invisible to my eyes, used a pair of tweezers to extract them. Then he has scrutinised his face in the rear-view mirror, and commenced the unpleasant and unsociable process again.

After about four hours of this I have given up trying to divert him with conversation and have gazed out at jungle and fields, wild orchids by the roadside, the ragged thatched huts in rain-splattered paddies of rice, and a military base protected by walls and barbed-wire.

But the discomforts of bearing witness to Richard's grooming are going to be worth this drive because—after my sweat-drenched up-river journey later, from a slippery landing beneath the shabby village of Sebeliau—will be a longhouse of the Iban people.

Within the living memory of their elders these people were headhunters, a practice most texts say ended in the 1930s. But Japanese soldiers fleeing Kuching at the end of the Second World War fell to arrows and blow-darts poisoned by the sap of the Ipoh tree, and then the cutting blade of the people of this region.

Indeed, three blackened skulls hang in a basket from a roof beam in the Serubah longhouse which holds 20-odd families and around 200 people. The families here share a common area which disappears towards a distant point lost in the darkness inside the wooden walls.

I am the only visitor to this longhouse and Richard
tells me that today among these people the young have
embraced Christianity. Kitsch blonde *Jesus 90210* re-
productions on the wall of some homes within the longhouse attest to this—but many of the older folk still
observe traditional practices.

I am introduced to Unting, the shaman. He is a
wiry, witty (at least in translation) and wise-looking 87-
year old who cheerfully explains his many blue tattoos:
the traditional hibiscus flowers and the facing hornbills
on his upper chest because they are the symbols of
Sarawak, the snake on his leg came from three years
on Sabah to the north.

"Rain all time, long time," he says through Richard.
"Because I have no things to do I have these."

He laughs and points to the thick markings beneath
his chin and down his throat. They are for protection,
he says with a warm smile, but were the most painful.

He   shuffles   off   and   returns   with   tattoo
instruments—darning needles tied to the end of a
stick which are tapped into the flesh much as it done
in Samoa.

He holds them in his horny, blue-veined hands with
all the gentleness one might present a rare feather.

Later a handsome and lean man also in his 80s introduces himself. He is so revered that Richard, who
speaks this dialect, refers to him only as Tuairumah,
chief of the house.

When Tuairumah shakes my hand I can't help notice the large and expensive-looking watch on his other

wrist.

He tells me I am welcome in the place of his people, and they are pleased to share what they have.

And that seems considerable. The land around the longhouse is productive: corn, bananas, cucumber, the ever important betel nut still favoured by the old people, the distinctive black Sarawak pepper seeds which are drying in the heat of the afternoon sun on the long veranda, rubber tapped from trees. . .

Blue-brown smoke across the river, rising as a massive and menacing cloud, drops flecks of ash on the longhouse all afternoon—and is evidence of an another important crop. And a problem with the neighbours.

All through this region local people are felling and burning the jungle to plant fields of rice, a rotation crop which accounts for those sudden clearings on the journey up-river.

By nightfall the sky has an insipid yellow glow above the jungle canopy and the women in the longhouse are engaging in an animated discussion.

It seems people from nearby longhouses are burning the nearby jungle for a rice field but haven't asked their permission. The consensus among the womenfolk is that Tuairumah and others will need to have a council with them.

There is much gesturing—the headman's wife the most visibly agitated. She talks at her husband for many uninterrupted minutes then leaves.

The old man looks weary as we drink fermented rice wine. Women and children disappear behind the rattan walls to their homes, the old men sit and sip.

There is much nodding and head-shaking but very little is verbalised. I nod too. They nod at me, an accepted stranger in their company.

This longhouse has another source of income beyond crops: an increasing stream of buses from Kuching bring tourists into this region.

Late in the day while swimming with the children I have seen groups of middle-aged, camera-laden visitors in the narrow boats ploughing up the swiftly flowing Lemanak to other longhouses on this stretch of the river.

The children wave furiously and smile their grills of perfect teeth, and have their photographs taken by zoom lenses. Maybe back home in Berlin or Boston as they recall their trip up the dirty river these visitors might look at their photographs and wonder who that strange white face amongst the nut-brown children belongs to.

It isn't a comfortable journey up-river, the Lemanak can be unforgiving: sudden eddies appear, there are patches of ominous calm, huge tree stumps rear out of it dramatically at odd angles, and there are unpredictable depths and shallows judging by areas where the surface churns for no apparent reason.

As we sit on the veranda in the strength-sapping humidity Richard tells me of the four German tourists in a longboat which capsized: the two women managed to hold onto low vines until they were rescued—but the two men had raincoats over their life-jackets and were dragged down the river.

Their bodies were found three days later and the

Iban wouldn't use this important section of their river until a shaman could release the troubled spirits.

These ancient practices appear to remain uncompromised by tourism. Although the desultory performance of the hornbill dance for my sole benefit by the headman, another old fellow, and two women—all in traditional costume and accompanied by a small orchestra of women playing tuned gongs—suggests that culture and commerce now co-exist uneasily.

I am more comfortable when Tuairumah simply sits and we drink rice wine afterwards, none of us saying much.

By saying less I learn more: the mats covered in cultural takeaways—masks, carvings and the like—which are neatly displayed on yellowed newspapers on the longhouse floor for tourist consumption aren't made by these people. They come from Indonesian artisans across the border who work cheaper. It seems I am witness to a microcosm of globalisation.

And the Iban today, somewhat surprisingly given their seemingly remote location, have cellphone coverage—although admittedly limited. In Tuairumah's living room the large lounge suite is still wrapped in plastic and he owns an impressively sized television.

Other aerials jut out of the roof at strange angles.

Late at night when we are making for bed Unting shakes my hand hard and, unprompted, tells me again they like visitors.

In accordance with tribal tradition, guests are encouraged to bring gifts for the longhouse and on the way here I have been guided by Richard as to what is appropriate.

We pulled in at a small marketplace-cum-lunchstop for buses and he bought a large plastic bag containing 40 packets of instant noodles, and bags of lollies for the children.

I wondered aloud about the appropriateness of these but he is insistent and says the children will be delighted.

I said I didn't doubt it, and he is confused by my discomfort at these "gifts" and what I see will be the inevitable consequences of lollies and instant noodles— which I later suspect were traded back to the shop where tourists such as myself buy them. If so, then this is perhaps a trading convenience and social gesture in which everyone wins, and the kids seem delighted, as I expected, to see the lolly bag I carry.

The children seem like kids anywhere: the boys and I flounder in the river using balloons and an inner tube as cheap flotation devices, others take hours of pleasure with handmade kites and run the length of the veranda hauling them into the ash-filed air.

It is still officially the dry season but a deafening seven hour downpour which drops into the impenetrable black of night at 3 AM gives the lie to that.

It is unimaginable what it might be like here in the jungle during monsoon season when torrential rain will fall for days, if not weeks, and the Lemanak will rise three or four metres.

Even on this saturating morning which washes the blue-brown sky clean but leaves the air rank with the smell of rotting vegetation, the river climbs measurably up its banks and the incessant warm rain turns rivulets into torrents. My "nature walk" which Richard has threatened is mercifully cancelled. Everyone stays indoors except for an old man who shows me how to use a blowpipe.

Later I sit in a doorway watching the fighting cocks huddle in the corner of their pens as a longboat of tourists wrapped up against the downpour bounces past, slapping against the roiling, muddying water of the Lemanak.

When Richard and I prepare to leave for Sebeliau in a couple of longboats helmed by semi-naked men from the village, we strip down to our underwear and put our clothes and shoes in plastic bags.

Tomorrow, Richard says, a tour group of about 20 English tourists—carrying noodles and lollies I suppose—is coming here from the new Hilton Batang Ai Longhouse Resort.

It is just 30 minutes away from the muddy clearing below Sebeliau where we got into the longboat to come up-river and meet these people in what was once a remote corner of Sarawak on the border of Indonesian Borneo.

As we watch the river rise I can't help think: The horror! The horror!

Apocalypse soon.

Heaven's Highway

(Mississippi, USA)

ONE OF THE guidebooks wasn't especially helpful when it came to scenery. Then again, something entitled *Rock'n'Roll Traveler USA* was always going to be more interested in directing you to the field in which Buddy Holly's plane crashed, or the Taliesyn Ballroom in Tennessee where the Sex Pistols played the second concert of their notorious and short US tour in 78. The latter is now a Taco Bell incidentally.

These are interesting places for rock music aficionados such as myself to be sure, but most are hardly worth the diversion. However when we read a rare mention of something as un-hip as "a nice drive" we are immediately besotted.

"Farther south is Jackson, the state capital," it says in the chapter about Mississippi where we are headed, "connected to Tupelo by the Natchez Trace, one of the nation's loveliest drives".

Well, we are aiming our rental up from New Orleans in Louisiana to Natchez on the banks of the mighty and muddy Mississippi. After that we were planning to go on through the Delta and blues country to Tupelo in the north east corner of Mississippi to see the birthplace of Elvis Presley, where our book would surely become more handy.

But this small aside about one of America's loveliest drives sounds too tempting to miss. If authors Tim Perry and Ed Glinert—who could point you to such minutiae as Madame Marie's boardwalk hut in New Jersey's Asbury Park area, as mentioned in Bruce Springsteen's song *Fourth of July*—thought this a drive worth doing then we were hardly going to argue. These people had obviously seen a lot of America's highways and low roads so must know what they are talking about.

"So, y'all goin' to Tupelo?" says Mike in a small but rowdy bar in Natchez. He's shouting over the basketball commentary on the radio and the dozen or so patrons who are rooting for a hometeam win.

I nod as we are joined by his friend Ray carrying more beers.

"Man, you gotta drive the Trace," he bellows, "Prettiest piece of road in the whole damn country."

It is now mid-evening and we have arrived in Natchez that afternoon. We have driven the quiet streets and at the visitor's centre have picked up brochures for some of the stately homes around the town which rest in quiet gardens under dogwoods and oaks dripping with Spanish Moss.

It is all very delightful and Natchez, the oldest permanent settlement on the Mississippi River, is where the cotton plantation owners lived while keeping their properties across the river in Louisiana. It is cooler up on the Natchez bluff than the vast and low flatlands on the other side so here are glorious antebellum homes of the kind familiar from *Gone With the Wind*.

Prior to the Civil War over half the millionaires in the United States lived in Natchez and—because the town wasn't a military target—most of the 500 homes, churches and public buildings constructed in the Greek Revival style have remained intact.

They boast grand and graceful names like Stanton Hall—five levels of rooms built in 1857—and Longwood, which is octagonal and topped by a Moorish-style dome.

"So y'all seen Longwood then?" says Mike. "Terrible tragedy that story, but then again most of them old plantation owners never lived much to enjoy the homes they built."

He's right: Haller Nutt who built Longwood picked a bad time to start construction on his enormous six floor structure. Building began on the family mansion in 1860 and the following year the Civil War broke out. Ever the businessman, Nutt tried to placate both sides as his builders and craftsmen fled or joined the Northern troops. But when the Union army marched into Natchez they had no sympathy for him even though he had provided comfort for their troops. They destroyed his stock-piled cotton then valued at over US$1 million. We can only imagine what that might have meant in today's money.

Nutt and his family had finished only the base-ment rooms of Longwood and that was where he died— they say of a broken heart although the diagnosis was pneumonia—three years later.

The owner of Stanton Hall didn't have much bet-ter luck. He died in 1859 shortly after his magnificent mansion was completed. His family remained there for another 35 years, rattling around in a home which boasted six bedrooms on the second floor and has three reception rooms off the 30 metre entrance hallway.

These days many of the old homes of Natchez are administered by the Pilgrimage Garden Club, southern belles who often dress in period costume of layered pet-ticoats and are only too happy to guide visitors around them and tell the stories of the homes' histories.

One of these gentle docents had conducted us around Stanton Hall, her petticoats rustling in the cool breeze as we step onto the terrace.

There is another history in Natchez of course, that of the slaves who worked and died for King Cotton. The rundown Natchez Museum of Afro-American His-tory and Culture on Main St is the necessary corrective after enjoying the elegance of the mansions.

Here in the former post office another, more tragic, story unfolds. The gap between this threadbare mu-seum scraping for donations and the preserved and re-stored homes of the slave owners speaks of a divide not yet bridged.

But in the Corner Bar at Canal and State a conversation about the history of this town doesn't mean much when the home-team is down a few points. Mike and Ray can't stop extolling the virtues of the Natchez Trace. Both travel up to Nashville frequently and most times if they aren't in a hurry they'll drive the Trace, despite the low speed limit imposed.

"Feels like you're just takin' a quiet flight if you travel up that way," says Mike. "Y'all should check it out."

"Natchez Trace" is the old French name given to the 800 kilometre trail between Natchez and Nashville in Tennessee first "traced out" by buffalo, and then by the Indians who began following them around 8000 years ago. It was known to the Chickasaws as "the path of peace" and in their wake came trappers and missionaries.

In 1733 it began appearing on French maps of the region, and on British charts was known as "the path to the Choctaw nation".

By the early 19th century this was the main route home for those up-state traders who had floated their wares downriver to New Orleans but wisely preferred to undertake the return overland journey north rather than battle the treacherous and unpredictable eddies and currents of the Mississippi.

The Trace wasn't without it's dangers however: it ran through land belonging to two Indian nations and the forest was home to poisonous snakes, thick swamp and bandits who could quickly appear from the dark trees. It became known as the Devil's Backbone.

But as river transport improved the trail was less favoured and inevitably Nature took back its own. A century ago the Natchez Trace had all but disappeared.

Then the local chapter of the Daughters of the American Revolution campaigned to have it reopened and the smooth two-lane highway which follows the old trail was established.

And this is where we are headed the following morning after a noisy night in the bar, with the disappointment of a home-team loss and Ray's suggestion ringing in our ears: "Check out the Natchez Indian museum just outside of town before you go. You won't regret it."

The museum, a tiny place which recounts how these sun-worshippers were wiped out within a decade or so of the arrival of European explorers, is set near the old burial mounds and fields they tended. It is possessed of a holy silence and afterwards we remain quiet in the car as we head toward the connection with the Trace which briefly runs parallel to Highway 61, made famous in popular culture by a young and electrifying Bob Dylan. Which is mentioned in our rock'n'roll guidebook, of course.

As with the burial ground, the gentle contours and camber of Trace impose an emotional quietness on us.

The car set on slow cruise-control glides through leafy glades and patches of open grassland, over small bridges which ford glistening streams, through dark almost impenetrable patches of cypress forest.

The ribbon of the road stretches around easy curves, the inclines of the highway leaning lazily into the landscape. Beyond the dogwoods are ancient sites and walking trails, Indian burial grounds and Confederate graves, and the remnants of abandoned villages. History is breathing here.

We explore small trails, and stop to let an armadillo hop across the road in front of us and disappear into the forest. Out there are deer and squirrels as well as copperheads, cottonmouths and rattlers.

Later we pull over and do nothing but listen to wind in the trees, watch wide oceans of pale grass ripple in the breeze and feel the sense of this vast, unending land stretch out beyond the dark trees on the skyline, beyond our vision, beyond our imagination.

In the early 80s the Sioux writer William Least Heat Moon wrote about the Natchez Trace in his autobiographical travel book *Blue Highways*: "Now new road, opening the woods again, went in among redbuds and white blossoms of dogwood, curving about under a cool evergreen cover. For miles no powerlines or billboards. Just tree, rock, water, bush, and road.

"The new Trace, like a river, follows the natural contours and gave focus to the land; it so brought out the beauty that every road commissioner in the nation should drive the Trace to see that highway does not have to outrage landscape."

We watch clouds brush the blue sky above this American Arcadia. I put aside the maps and brochures we have been given. Nature here is the text, the defining document of this landscape. Its flesh is these low hills, its arteries the trenches worn into the soil where ancient tribes and buffalo once walked.

Sophisticated Man swishing past in motor vehicles cannot improve on this landscape and so, in a rare moment of wisdom, he has left it alone and let it be, if nothing else, one of the most exquisite roads in America.

We drive on in silence.

Nashville, country music and rowdy bars lie a very long way up this restful road.

The Road Less Travelled

(California, USA)

BILL FOSTER NEVER saw an animal he didn't like. And like so much that he would shoot the thing, have it's head chopped off and stuffed, and brought back to his bar in smalltown Rio Vista, halfway between San Francisco and Sacramento where he could admire it at his leisure.

While most travellers hit Interstate 80 and speed between San Francisco's Bay Bridge to California's capital in a couple of hours, there is a more rewarding journey down the old roads.

This route goes through small towns and past places like Bill Foster's Bighorn Saloon, a long bar where the walls are lined with those preserved heads and photos of Bill going about his manly work.

Bill had been a bootlegger and came to this town on the Sacramento River in 1931 to start anew as a legitimate bar owner after Prohibition ended in '33. Earlier in life he'd become excited by big game when he'd been an apprentice in a factory owned by Henry Snow, a hunter who brought back movies of African wildlife in 1918.

Bill was as enthusiastic about taxidermy and photography as he was about hunting and killing. He made dozens of trips to Africa, Alaska and Canada and recorded his triumphs faithfully on film, and in the flesh by taking with him some favourite taxidermists.

Bill wasn't content with rabbits or even moose. His California-backwater bar and restaurant contains the heads of an African elephant (the largest mammal trophy in any collection anywhere they say) and a white rhino. They are there alongside zebras, tigers and lions, and even the head and long neck of a giraffe.

There are more than 300 wild animals, birds and fish here from every part of the world that Bill travelled to and shot his way through.

A lampstand on the bar is an elephant's foot, under the rack of spirit bottles is a 9kg trout. There is fur, flesh, tusks and horns everywhere. The t-shirts they sell boast Foster's as "the horniest saloon in the west".

The bar snack speciality is, unusually in this palace of animal flesh, deep fried asparagus—presumably from nearby Isleton which once enticingly billed itself as "The Asparagus Capital of the West".

In the restaurant at the rear however—where diners sit beneath the disconcerting heads of that elephant and giraffe—the special of the day is usually beefburger. I didn't see a vegetarian option.

Bill retired from big game hunting in 1953 and devoted himself to working in the bar which had supported his habit. The elephant head was the last he hung up.

Vegans and anti-animal cruelty people might hope for some irony here, that the effort of placing this mammoth trophy on his wall might have killed him. But life isn't like that.

Bill died a decade later—but the Bighorn Saloon is his legacy, and is a popular watering hole for hunters and the curious. It's a safe bet you haven't seen anything like it.

Foster's is one of the odder highlights on the more leisurely and interesting drive to Sacramento, the first part of which follows the customary Highway 80 route until the turnoff to Fairfield about halfway along.

By this time freeway driving may have palled so it is time to turn off to the Delta. And yes, California has a Delta just like Mississippi.

In fact the Delta land around the Sacramento River was where *The Adventures of Huckleberry Finn* was filmed in 1960. Producer Sam Goldwyn Jnr claimed it looked "more like the Mississippi than the real thing".

Tiny Rio Vista is the gateway to the California Delta and lies down the road from Travis Airforce Base where huge cargo planes lumber through the blue sky and the road is lined with little boxes made of ticky-tacky in estates for the military and their families.

By Rio Vista, however, that ugly new world imposed on the landscape has dropped away and the road rides a single lane on top of the levee where the roofs of houses and the Mississippi's doppelganger, the winding Sacramento, are beneath on each side.

This is an easy country drive with little traffic and a lot to look at: walnut groves (up ahead is the town of Walnut Grove), jays flitting through the pear trees, and 19th century towns which have been all but abandoned.

The route runs parallel to the Sacramento River and ghostly quiet Isleton (yes, still "The Asparagus Capital of the West") offers the first taste of what happens to towns when the folks up and leave.

Main Street is, for the most part, lined with abandoned shops and wooden storefronts. This was once a Chinatown (Hop Fat and Co. is a prominent building) and home to those imported workers who built the levees which keep the floodwaters off the rich surrounding farmland.

There is a laughably small "casino".

In June however you'll struggle to find parking. That's when Isleton hosts the annual crawfish festival. Further along is Ryde, so small it barely registers, where actor Lon Chaney Jnr once owned the now-restored Grand Island Inn.

Of more interest however is Locke some 15 minutes away. Built in 1912 by Chinese workers it is a town sliding quietly into oblivion.

The battered wooden stores with their peeling paint and fire damage along the side of the road are just the front, the real town lies one street back and below.

Here the two-storey buildings are so aged that they can barely hold themselves upright and many are on a precarious lean. If there are people in Locke they don't wish to make their presence known.

All the shops and the small museum are closed on this weekday afternoon, and a family sitting on their upstairs veranda scuttles back inside when they see us walking down the dusty and narrow Main Street.

The population of fewer than 70 is invisible and only Al-the-Wop's, the bar, seems to be doing any trade. A couple of bikers pull up and go inside to quench their thirsts.

One guide book says Locke is becoming a tourist destination full of knick-knack shops but there is scant evidence of that. Just shops which have dusty window displays and doors which look like they are seldom opened.

A lone dog trots on Main Street.

Locke is a strange, silent place which is just a few dozen people away from being a ghost town.

Beyond Locke the road passes through Courtland, again below the levee and notable for a handsome bank with Greek columns.

Time and haste have passed these places by. This is pear country and it works to slower rhythms, much like the Mississippi Delta to which it bears such a strong resemblance.

It is difficult now, as you wend along deserted roads where the Sacramento make its slow, muddy way through the landscape, to believe this region was vibrant with life. These sleepy backwaters were once served by steamboats packed with those in search of fortunes in gold and then, when that proved an illusion, in the more practical opportunities of orchards and farms.

Paddle-wheelers and scows once plied these dust brown waters and pulled up at the numerous docks along the route, now mostly used by recreational fishers. Houseboats have replaced schooners.

Today signs have an ironic and amusing ring to them: who'd have though they be driving through central California and see a sign which could, in all truth, proclaim "Delta Blues Barn"?

The road meanders easily along the levee then slowly, almost imperceptibly, becomes one with modern America again.

We are suddenly out of tree-lined road and fragrant orchards and into noisy and self-interested Sacramento by a back door, once more in the world of wide freeways, motels, fast-food options, Adopt-A-Highway signs and self-serve petrol stations.

Back there is the road less bothered with, abandoned somewhere in the mid 20th century—and its people prefer it that way.

Of course some make the trip in reverse. A few days later we considered that, but it might mean a late lunch at Foster's Bighorn Saloon and we didn't much care to be chomping through beef steak while being watched by a mournful moose, some decapitated deer, and that grey elephant.

Or the giraffe, neck and all.

Islamistan in Alohaland

(Honolulu, The Hawaiian Islands)

�֍

AT THE END of a fascinating and sometimes scandalous life, the American heiress and socialite Doris Duke was unlikely to go into that great goodnight without some attendant controversy—and she didn't disappoint.

When she died in 1993 at one of her homes—the so-called "Falcon's Lair" in Beverly Hills which had belonged to Rudolph Valentino—she left her billion dollar fortune to her charitable foundation. The catch was it would be administered by her loyal butler Bernard Lafferty, a mildly eccentric, gay Irishman most often described as a drunkard and semi-literate.

There were persistent allegations—although Duke was 80 and had suffered heart problems and a series of strokes—that "the butler did it" because the protective Lafferty, who kept family and friends away in the last years of Duke's life, was at her bedside and she was cremated within a day.

But long before speculation about her death was Duke's singular life: she inherited a fortune at age 12 and was dubbed by the press "the Million Dollar Baby"; had two brief, high-profile marriages and serial lovers; and in 1988 at age 75 she adopted a 35-year old former bellydancer and Hare Krishna devotee with whom some believed she was in a lesbian relationship. Always conscious of her looks—in her early life she was tall, tanned, and angular in an athletic way with a prominent chin—she had a facelift at 79.

With colourful locations, money to fritter and the backdrop of 20th century events and public figures, Duke's life could be read as a script for a brash movie.

And indeed there has been a recent film made about her final days, *Bernard and Doris* starring Ralph Fiennes and Susan Sarandon. There was also a television mini-series in the late 90s with Lauren Bacall as Duke and Richard Chamberlain as Lafferty.

Certainly the breadth of Duke's life—alleged affairs with actor Errol Flynn, Hawaiian surf champion and Olympic swimmer Duke Kahanamoku, and General Patton among others—was made for the motion picture screen. But as Norma Desmond observed in Sunset Boulevard, the pictures got small.

And Doris Duke's life was big.

Aside from gossip, lovers and a fortune, Duke left a more publicly tangible legacy—her home on the Hawaiian island of Oahu near Waikiki Beach which she built in the late Thirties. In recent years it has been opened to small groups of visitors.

Few tourists who hit the bars, beaches and aloha-shirt shops on Oahu make it to Duke's oceanfront house. It is under-publicised and only 12 visitors at a time are allowed entry on four days a week. The curious must book in advance.

The modest gateway in the suburban street suggests nothing of what lies beyond. Her house, Shangri La as she called it, is all but invisible as you come down the driveway to the main entrance which is simply wooden doors in a featureless wall without windows. Only the two stone camels from China at the entrance hint at the pleasure palace within.

Duke—who owned homes and apartments in New York, Rhode Island and Los Angeles as well as a farm in New Jersey—considered the five-acre property and Shangri La her retreat.

"Doris Duke liked her privacy," says Charles, the softly-spoken guide who is showing just two mainland couples and me around on this typically warm day. "You will have noted that when you came down the driveway, this is a very private house."

Even when seen from passing boats little of Shangri La reveals itself, its discreet low lines offer no hint of its inner opulence or overtly announce its unusual contents.

What makes Shangri La so interesting is that—as with William Randolph Hearst's mountain-top eyrie in California—it is a monument to unconstrained wealth, eclectic taste, restless acquisition and eccentricity.

However unlike Hearst's baroque conflation of architecture and art from all over the globe, Duke's home—with a stunning view of the Pacific and Diamond Head—has a more singular focus: in this quiet suburb of Ka'alawai her house is a spacious and sometimes restful mix of... of all things, Islamic art and design.

Stepping through that wooden door inscribed in Arabic "enter here in peace and security" you walk into a world which is lavish yet elegantly minimal.

Over there are 17th century ceramic tiles from Turkey, down there in the inner courtyard around the fountain are some from 13th century Iran, here a light fixtures from Syria and there a mosaic made by Duke in 1938 based on Iranian arabesques.

Through here is the enormous living room and note how, although this house is rooted in the past and other more exotic places, Duke utilised modern technology of her time: that glass wall of maybe 12 metres in width and perhaps five metres high can slide down into the floor at the push of a button.

Now you have an unimpeded view of Diamond Head beyond the Olympic-size pool where Buster Crabbe and Johnny Weissmuller once swam.

In her will Duke bequeathed this place to her foundation to "promote the study and understanding of Middle eastern art and culture", a lofty aim but ...

Shangri La is evidence that Duke didn't curate, she decorated. And this was a home not a gallery. Duke saw what she liked, bought it and then placed it where it suited her. Although it draws on Islamic art—whatever that might mean given the diversity of it through various countries—there is no cultural consistency beyond what was aesthetically pleasing to her.

One large mosaic of illustrative tiles is placed on a wall sideways because it better suited the view down the hallway. The undeniably exquisite 13th century mihrab—a wall niche indicating the direction of Mecca —rather than facing northwest is on an eastern wall. It simply looked better there—and, religious considerations aside, she was probably right.

Elsewhere separate centuries and styles are juxtaposed.

And in it's heyday Duke had Hawaiian knick-knacks and household objects—hula-girl glasses, surfboards— around the place. This was a home to be lived in, not admired with the objective eye of a scholar.

Her collection of some 3500 items is where the real treasure for a scholar might lie, but to peruse those you need special permission.

However Shangri La, just as any home which bears the bold fingerprint of its occupants, rewards a visit on its own terms.

This is where Duke lived—when she wasn't travelling in search of adventure or artefacts. Or living in one of her other homes such as that at Newport, Rhode Island where, after a controversial accident in 1966 in which she killed her interior decorator Eduardo Tirella, she founded a restoration society to maintain and restore some of the town's old buildings.

Many said the gesture was Duke buying off the bad publicity, but that is perhaps unfair. All her life she was given to philanthropy, and she certainly had a lot to give from a bottomless well of money.

Doris' father James "Buck" Duke made his millions from tobacco, property and energy companies and when he died in 1935 she inherited the majority of his estate. It was, when paid in full, something more than a billion dollars in today's money.

The young Doris was by all accounts a smart and intelligent child, and although her wealth allowed her to indulge various passions such as a love of animals (she was a devout vegetarian), the arts and travel, she was far from frivolous with her money. As her third cousin, the improbably named Pony Duke, noted, "She didn't have hobbies, she had obsessions and she turned all her interests into businesses".

She made many and large donations to charities.

But she also took care of her own increasingly rapacious desires, and when she married James Cromwell in 1935 the couple went on a lengthy honeymoon which took them to—among other places—India, where she fell in love with the Taj Mahal.

She immediately commissioned a marble bedroom based on designs and motifs of that exotic tomb which she intended to have constructed in the couple's Florida home.

The final stop on their 10-month honeymoon was Hawaii. The relaxed pace and tropical climate won her over and she and James stayed four months. Plans for the Florida home were put on hold and she began to conceive of a retreat on the picturesque property at Ka'alawai which she purchased.

And so, with more than 100 local workers and from

designs by the architect Marion Sims Wyeth, building
began immediately and the home was occupied in late
1938.

But it was always a work in progress and even late
in life Duke—who was hands-on and would lay tiles
herself—kept adding, redesigning and changing the location of pieces.

She used Shangri La—named for the Utopian king-
dom in James Hilton's pre-war escapist novel *Lost
Horizon*—as a seasonal retreat, more so after she and
James divorced in 1943.

Although she was busy with the house Duke also
had time for life. She was briefly married to the notorious playboy-cum-diplomat Porfirio Rubirosa in 1947, a
man equally hedonistic and so well-endowed that waiters referred to the pepper grinder as "the Rubirosa".
Duke described his penis as "six inches in circumfer-
ence... much like the last foot of a Louisville Slugger
baseball bat".

She entertained herself with travel, alcohol and
drugs, playing jazz piano, numerous lovers, parties and
famous guests—who were accommodated in the pil-
lared luxury of the "Playhouse" beyond the pool at
Shangri La. When on the island she surfed competi-
tively and for pleasure—and pleasure, especially of the
sexual kind, was something she knew well as a few sala-
cious biographies attest.

Charles, our guide, is circumspect to the point of
looking dyspeptic when I ask whether there is a thor-
ough biography of Doris Duke. He leaves us in no doubt
that bad press and innuendo about Duke remains out-

side those wooden doors.

He does note however that late in life she had fewer and fewer friends call, although he doesn't mention Lafferty's well-publicised part in keeping visitors out.

As her health deteriorated the fiercely loyal, binge-drinking, barefooted and pony-tailed Lafferty—who sported a butler's uniform but took to wearing Doris' designer dresses after her death and cruising gay clubs in Los Angeles—ensured the former society queen was kept in something approaching seclusion.

Ironically Duke had grown up in much the same manner, her father fearful of his daughter being kidnapped meant she travelled everywhere with bodyguards. Trust no one, he famously warned her as a child.

At the end she was left with Lafferty, her beloved dog—she made a provision for care of both in a will which also noted Imelda Marcos owed her US$5 million from an outstanding loan when she'd posted the Marcos" bail. And at Shangri La, she had eclectic Islamic décor in a European modernist building on a balmy Pacific island.

Tellingly she referred to the patchwork style of Shangri La as "Hispano-Mooresque" and "Near Eastern", descriptions which more fairly reflect the pastiche of art and architectural influences. In her idiosyncratic way Doris Duke may have been an early post-Modernist.

Hawaiians are not unfamiliar with collisions of cultures: the social and political history of the island aside, this is a tropical place where Santa on a surfboard isn't uncommon at Christmas while the radio plays "Oh the weather outside is frightful... Let it snow, let it snow, let it snow".

So the conceit of an imagined Islamistan in the suburb of Ka'alawai isn't really so surprising. But Shangri La, like its creator, is unique.

When the house was nearing completion in 1938 a reporter for the *Honolulu Star Bulletin* wrote: "On all the face of the globe there is no other place like it, nor is there likely to be."

And at that time Doris Duke hadn't even brought in most of the Islamic décor—or the pet leopard.

Let's Get Lost

(California, USA)

❋

MID-AFTERNOON ON A weekday in the 21 Club, a bar in the rundown Tenderloin district of San Francisco with a handwritten sign which reads "No bicycles inside" on the battered glass door.

Outside broken and damaged people push supermarket trolleys of their belongings past cheap strip joints and rundown hotels, others mutter to themselves, and pan-handlers slump in doorways extending grubby hands towards anyone passing by. Police sirens strafe the urine-heavy air, and junkie-whores are more common than lampposts or dog-pissed fire hydrants.

We had been in America for less than two hours and when I arrived at the forsaken 21 Club place it was by unhappy but instructive accident.

I swear to God, but the first thing we bought after getting off the plane after the 12-hour flight was booze and a mix: a small bottle of Bombay Sapphire gin and some Minute Maid pink lemonade from a Korean liquor store on the corner of Third and Townsend.

There was a good reason of course—not that you need a reason—but we needed money for the parking meter.

We'd hired a car at the airport and driven into Downtown. It was only early afternoon and despite that half-day in an airborne cocoon I thought we could check out the Museum of Cartoon Art at 665 Third St. I'd hauled the car over into the first space I saw on the way up Third and there, directly opposite, was 665.

Even closer was the parking meter.

I had ATM bills in 10s, 20s and 100s, but no small change. So I went to the nearest place I saw, the Korean liquor store.

As it happened the museum had moved but at least we were provisioned.

And, embarrassing as it is to admit, the next thing we bought was beer in the shabby 21 Club.

We had driven through the Tenderloin district with its strip clubs and panhandlers, where toothless men slept on the footpath or in their wheelchairs, and dropped the car in a parking building. We started walking. Past girlie bars and all-nude review joints, past hookers in acrid smelling alleys, and past the helpless and the homeless.

I needed to pee so we went into the first bar we saw, the 21 Club. It was a haven for the hopeless: a guy asleep across the wall seats, sloppy drunks and whores on a break, the maniac with the rolling eyes...

I loved it.

The 21 Club was only as interesting as such places always are: an impressive collection of tawdry souvenirs (fungal-stained plastic dolls, an African mask which could have been made in Taiwan, team pennants and sports memorabilia) and there was a collection of books beneath the Myers Rum and Jack Daniels' bottles. It included dictionaries of baseball statistics and movies, and a *World Almanac* (1953 edition). These were doubtless used to settle arguments.

That said, the guy asleep on the small wall seats in the corner didn't look like he was in a mood to argue about anything, or even have a coherent conversation. Nor did the bearded white guy who looked like he'd fought in the hippie wars 40 years ago and lost.

His conversation rambled and it was all pretty forgettable, until he complained about his tumour.

"The doctor says I should get it seen to as soon as possible. It's the size of a fist and all the skin over it is pulling real tight now."

He didn't offer where this invasive thing was located on his anatomy, but got up to feed the jukebox.

He chose the blues song *Last Fair Deal* and a version of Little Feat's *Willin'*, the lyrics of which in part run: "I've been warped by the rain, driven by the snow, I'm drunk and dirty and don't you know, that I'm still willin'."

That seemed appropriate.

"Hey! You workin'?" yelled the wild-eyed guy who lurched up to me menacingly, then laughed and rolled his eyes some more. I laughed too, nervously, and he shuffled off.

Tumourman came back and with great effort pulled his substantial belly and bum back on the bar stool and ordered up another red wine. He started talking again, but my attention wandered to the guy in the other corner who kept asking the pleasant barman the time, and if he could have just a little more water in his tumbler of whisky. He was making his drink last a long time.

No bad thing actually, there was nothing to do back on those deadbeat, fag-end streets anyway.

But we were different. Alone among this company we did have places to go and people to meet.

I finished my beer, made my farewells through handshakes, a backslap and absent waves to emotionally excused, then walked out of the 21 Club into the bright sunlight and the promise of a cloudless Northern California afternoon.

I left them all behind. But for days I carried with me the image of a tumour the size of a fist trying to escape the world-weary shell of a man with food scraps in his nicotine-stained beard.

Dealing in Dreams

(Golden Triangle, Thailand)

�֍

SIR JOHN BOWRING, Governor of Hong Kong for
six years in the mid-19th century, was one of those
damnable crackpot Christian capitalists of the kind we
just don't see any more: "Free trade is Jesus Christ,
and Jesus Christ is free trade," he once declaimed.

For the Governor and many of his politically powerful peers, British economic expansion into China went
hand in glove with Christianity. And opium.

Within two decades of opium being shipped from
poppy fields in the colony of India and sold into China
with the tacit approval of the British Government, the
balance of trade had shifted in Britain's favour. The
Chinese Government emptied its coffers of silver to buy
this powerfully addictive and enjoyably escapist drug
which was decimating its people.

163

Trade in opium was worth twice all other imports, but in 1839 the Chinese Government proclaimed the drug, and trade in it, illegal. And so the Opium Wars.

Bowring is a bit player in the long and complex history of opium in Asia—a drug identified as having curative properties as far back as ancient Sumeria and Egypt.

The pre-Renaissance physician Paracelcus is purported to have been the first to make laudanum—opium mixed with alcohol. Among its many addicts were Benjamin Franklin, the poet Samuel Taylor Coleridge, and countless millions from the docks of Liverpool to the slums of Shanghai.

Today the opium poppy—papaver somniferum, one of 250 species of poppy but the only one to produce the drug—is harvested in Afghanistan (again, after the Taliban regime banned it in 2000), Pakistan, Laos and Myanmar (Burma) to produce a cash crop for poor farmers.

In the notorious but scenic Golden Triangle where Myanmar, Thailand and Laos meet, opium growing was once the major economy and its trade enforced by powerful warlords such as Lo Hsing-han who, in 1972, boasted he was dealing 180 tons a year.

Though Laos and Myanmar are still alleged to have opium fields, Thailand has all but eradicated the growing of opium poppies (on pain of lengthy imprisonment). But it is fitting that the new Hall of Opium Museum should be in the Golden Triangle near the tiny town of Ban Sop Ruak. Just a kilometre from the Mekong River—with China 300km upriver and Laos on the far bank. The museum offers a special journey through the history of opium.

On a humid afternoon I walk the long driveway to its extraordinary rooms which are built right through a mountain. The young woman who greets me in the foyer seems mildly alarmed at my sudden appearance. I guess they don't have too many visitors, an instinct proven correct. I am the only one here today.

She hesitantly asks me to wait for reasons unspecified and so, with a thoughtfully provided Dixie cup of water, I read the brochure which fills in the background to this extraordinary place.

In 1988, Thailand's late Princess Mother recognised that the opium trade—which had only grown in the Golden Triangle in the previous half century—had become the cash economy for the various hill tribes. Theirs was a life of slash'n'burn in the jungle where they then planted poppy fields; the product of which would be bought by local warlords and their armies for sale around the region.

Her Royal Highness instigated development projects to give these hill people education and alternative sources of income, and encouraged research into the drug. The Hall of Opium offers a video introduction to the history of the trade and its effects on various societies.

But it is more than a museum of fascinating history, harrowing images and exotically beautiful and beguiling opium paraphernalia. It provides a literal and metaphoric journey from dark to light: from the long, dark entrance tunnel—where spotlights pick out wracked and ribbed bodies, and contorted faces carved into the wall—to the final room which is the Hall of Reflection with wise words from the *Talmud, Qur'an, the Bible,* Gandhi and other sources.

Tourism is now a money-spinner in this jungle region. Expensive and exquisite resorts with their spa retreats bring moneyed tourists here to enjoy the splendid isolation, balmy climate and views of three countries where the jungle refuses to acknowledge the borders.

The Anantara Resort and Spa—with its elephant camp and infinity pool—lies directly opposite the entrance to the Hall of Opium, and is tucked well into the canopy of bush and vines. The Greater Mekong Lodge is a stone's throw from the imposing entrance to the museum.

Visitors to this region can barely taste, let alone inhale, this dark part of Golden Triangle's history. A rare few sit in the small bars of untidy Ban Sop Ruak—which means "the village where rivers meet"—and sip beer and eat meals for less than $2 a plate. Most luxuriate in the spas and resorts hidden in the mist-covered jungle.

It's unlikely that traders still shift opium through here illicitly, but the Hall of Opium offers provocative deliberation about its exoticism and the price its victims have paid.

As I enjoy a cold beer in one of Ban Sop Ruak's bars built from cast-off corrugated-iron a single thought recurs: Sir John Bowring knew what free marketeers thought of opium, but he was silent on what Jesus Christ might have made of this trade in human misery.

Even in the Midst of Life

(Rome, Italy)

IT IS AN ODD juxtaposition. Just off Piazza Barberini in central Rome and only a short walk from the more famous Trevi Fountain is the Autocentri Balduini on Via Vittorio Veneto.

In its window glistening Lamborghini are displayed like glamorous mannequins in a high-end frock shop.

The proximity of other expensive retail outfits suggests you might just happen to come out of the nearby underground station, spot something yellow and low-slung of the Genus Automobile in the window which takes your fancy, and pop in to buy it on the credit card before going across the road for a panino.

Autocentri Balduini exudes speed and life and exoticism—and next door is a memento mori, a reminder that despite such temporal indulgences we are here for a very short time.

It is the Chiesa di Santa Maria della Concezione, and a part of it is the crypt for the remains of Capuchin monks.

It is one of the most unusual places in a marvellous city where the otherwise odd can often seem ordinary.

In five small chapels of the Chiesa are the skeletal remains of the monks who died between 1528 and 1870 have been arranged to form funerary art like no other.

Skulls and thigh bones are arranged to form altarpieces, vertebrae and ribs line up to create floral-style decorations, and a winged hourglass is made from shoulder blades.

Here is a crypt of pelvises, there another of skulls. In a passageway is a winged skull in a circular frame of vertebrae which appears to have angel wings: they too are shoulder blades. Elsewhere are skeletons where the tightly drawn mummified skin is still visible.

The Capuchin Chapel—entry by donation, no photographs, respectful silence please—was established around 1630 when monks moved from their former home near the Trevi Fountain to this new site, bringing with them the bones of their brethren. It is believed that some time in the late 1700s—when Capuchin friars fled persecution in France—the monks started to arrange the skeletal remains into the weirdly appealing designs we see today.

The peculiar thing about this ossuary is that within a few minutes those who make their way here suspend whatever ghoulishness may have brought them, and are in silent awe of the geometric constructions of vertebrae, a hanging lantern of sacral bones, and ribs arranged to make radiating patterns around a clock face formed from finger bones.

There is a theme here: that life is brief—the clock, the hourglass—and above the exit the inscription roughly translates to, "What I am now, you will become".

Gulp.

The chapel is a strangely compelling place which inspires a contemplation of mortality, and maybe even gives encouragement to live to the full the brief time we are given.

It might even prompt you to buy a yellow, low-slung Lamborghini from Autocentri Balduini next door in fact.

The Face of a Footnote

(Venice, Italy)

THE LANE LEADING from Venice's Piazza San Marco—the Merceria as it is called—is narrow and crowded. But it has always been so.

The Merceria was once the main thoroughfare in this city of eroding beauty and it remains the shortest route between San Marco and the Ponte di Rialto (the Rialto Bridge). That means teeming tourists, dozens of designer label stores, and seductively laid out shops selling glass from Murano.

And everywhere, of course, dozens of places filled with mass-produced miniatures of Carnival masks which John Berendt in his book *The City of Fallen Angels* notes have replaced local bakeries and butchers' shops. They are the "detested symbol of the city's capitulation to tourism at the expense of liveability".

Famous people have walked this winding path—Byron, Browning and Dickens definitely, scores of Antipodean and English television chefs no doubt, and various minor royals and politicians from all over Europe.

But while we know the course of history is often determined by the whims of politicians, kings and queens, it is commoners who put their shoulders to the wheel—and are more often than not the first to be crushed by it.

In the Merceria there is a small tribute to a commoner who performed an uncommon—and faintly absurd—act which altered the fate of Venice.

So, despite the press of people, I stop opposite an arch near San Marco and point out to my companions a small marble relief above us.

It is of Giustina Rosa and she is depicted leaning out of a window as if ready to drop some kind of pot on the heads of those passing below.

And once, she did exactly that.

Giustina was in the right place at the right time—and that time was June 15 1310, a date carved beneath her image and also set into the pavement beneath the tramping feet of our fellow tourists.

Giustina's original home is long gone of course, but her appearance—albeit very brief—in Venetian history has been immortalised in three dimensional marble. She leans forward past a curtain and what looks like a pot is actually a mortar balanced precipitously above the heads of passers-by.

Giustina Rosa's story is an unusual one.

Through some failure of natural succession and consequent instability in nearby Ferrara—today only an hour away—troops from Venice occupied that city. But Pope Clement V disapproved and gave the Venetian army 10 days to withdraw or Venice would be excommunicated.

Heated arguments broke out in Venice between those who feared the consequences (more financial than spiritual) and those who supported the Venetian Doge's defiance of the Pope.

However the Venetians occupying Ferrara were slaughtered by troops the Pope had called in, and back home some separate groups planned a concerted coup to oust the Doge.

One of the conspirators Bajamonte Tiepolo led his men down the Merceria towards the Doge's palace on the Piazza San Marco, taunted much of the way by civilians.

Tiepolo was within a few steps of St Mark's Square when old Giustina stepped into the pages of history. She leaned out her window and deliberately dropped her mortar. It hit Tiepolo's standard-bearer on the head and killed him. Tiepolo's proud standard fell to the ground.

Tiepolo, seeing some fatalistic symbolism in the moment, panicked and fled back down the Merceria, across the Ponte de Rialto—knocking it apart behind him—and holed up in his own district.

Concerned about civil disorder as some citizens rallied to hunt down Tiepolo, and others rose to his defence, the Doge negotiated a truce with Tiepolo. His home was torn down as part of the deal but at least he survived, unlike one of his co-conspirators who was beheaded.

And Giustina was handsomely rewarded.

Her landlords could not raise her rent, and her family could hang its banner on feast days from that famous window in perpetuity.

Well, perpetuity is a long time and her home— known as Casa della Grazia del Mortar—was pulled down over a century ago.

But Giustina Rosa's likeness—that of a broad shouldered old woman wrapped in a cloak and about to let loose her famous mortar—hovers over foot traffic in this part of the Merceria even today. Not that many notice.

Most are too busy peering into the expensive shops or jostling through the camera-wielding crowds making for San Marco or the Ponte di Rialto to look up and see the image of this woman, an uncommon commoner.

The Little Dictator

(Rome, Italy)

✳

ROME HADN'T SEEN anything like him before, this strutting little fanatic who was so gifted with words he could move a crowd to mass action.

A born propagandist, he was often invited into the homes of the wealthy for their amusement as they listened to him rant over the dinner table. But when he finally took complete power—without a hand raised against him—he ruled with ruthless authority.

Former dinner party hosts fled in terror.

Then the tide of history—and the people—tuned against him. After the mob tore him apart his body was hung upside down in ignominy.

Despite the broad familiarity of this story, this vain little man was not the fascist dictator Benito Mussolini, but Cola de Rienzi born 700 years ago and briefly the self-appointed "Tribune and Liberator of the Holy Roman Republic".

Rienzi's remarkably life barely makes a footnote in the history books, yet there is his statute on the Capitoline Hill by the steps to the right of the monument to Victor Emmanuel.

In stone, Rienzi cuts a peculiar figure: squat and oddly disproportionate, his face hidden by a hood, the right arm outstretched in some gesture of appeal or as if grasping something imaginary. The immortality he craved possibly? If so, this stone figure shows he achieved it.

In a city of statues, however, his is an unremarkable one and visitors to Victor Emmanuel invariably walk past it without a first, let alone a second, glance.

It is symptomatic of how a vibrant history informs every corner in this ancient city that Rienzi, who commanded Rome for a flamboyant, if brief, seven months should be so relegated in the imagination.

But his is an extraordinary story and one with resonances in modern fascism. In an echo across history Wagner's youthful opera *Rienzi*, about this mad despot and canny propagandist, impressed the young Adolph Hitler.

In later life Hitler is reported to have said his vision for the Third Reich was formed after having seen a production of the opera: "In that moment, it began."

Born around 1313 Rienzi was the son of a publican, but one who learned classical Latin. He wandered among the ruins dreaming of the glory of the Empire and imagining himself a Caesar.

At 30, he was sent by Rome's inn-keepers as an envoy to Avignon to congratulate the new pope, Clement VI, and beg him to return to Rome.

It seems the pope took a liking to this eloquent and handsome emissary and kept him around the palace for a year. When he finally returned to Rome Rienzi began secretly organising the citizenry to overthrow the nobility he so despised, to establish a peaceful, citizen-led state and, in a prescient vision, eventually a united Italy.

On the morning of May 20 1347 when many nobles were away from the city, the bell on the Capitol rang and the citizenry took to the streets in a planned uprising. Rienzi, in full armour and before a cheering crowd, declared his programme: murderers to be executed; roads made safe and robbers apprehended; all new law cases to be heard within 15 days; each district having its own home guard; and other such popular proposals.

He was given supreme power, returning nobles were forced to swear allegiance to him, and within a month he wrote to the Pope assuring him the streets and woods were safe. If Rienzi had lived in modern times doubtless he would have had trains running on time.

But his vanity was also unbridled: he would strut around in scarlet robes and golden spurs; devised his own elaborate coronation; and during a banquet suddenly arrested all the remaining nobles and had them prepared for execution. The following morning however he delivered them a speech on the virtues of forgiveness—and invited them to dinner. The nobles left vowing revenge.

Finally, even the citizenry wearied of the pomp and propaganda, and when the pope commanded they overthrow him, they rose up and Rienzi fled.

Curiously enough, this wasn't the last Rome saw of him. Seven years later the new pope, Innocent VI, saw in him a possible solution to the ongoing anarchy in Rome. Rienzi was dispatched back to city with a papal army.

But he was a much-changed man. Over-weight, penniless and dedicated to a programme of reform, he cajoled the citizens to greatness when they only wanted parties and pageantry. Fatally, he raised taxes.

For the second time the people rose up against him.

They dragged him to the steps of Santa Maria in Aracoeli where criminals were executed and for an hour he waited for someone to stick a blade into him. Cecco del Vecchio finally did the honours.

The body was strung up by the heels at San Marcello for two days and on the third cut down and burnt on a heap of thistles.

Rienzi's dramatic but short career is full of resonances of Mussolini and is instructive about the fickle nature of Romans.

But influential though he might have been, Rienzi's story is seldom talked about, even by guides who take their groups past his peculiar little statue.

To find out about him it is necessary to visit Rome in the company of an intelligent, witty and well-informed companion. Someone like the late HV Morton and more particularly his book *A Traveller in Rome* first published in 1957 in which the story of Rienzi is just one the fascinating minutiae this doyen of travel writers casually drops.

Henry Vollam Morton, a patrician Englishman who seldom invited the familiarity of being addressed by his Christian name, was born at the end of the 19th century and died in 1979.

He was a passionate traveller and wrote unassumingly intelligent and informative books: half a dozen about London; almost as many about his travels in the footsteps of Christ through what was then called the Holy Land; and on the roads St Paul walked.

His *In Search of...* series took him around Scotland, Ireland, South Africa, England and Wales. But Italy was his greatest love and on publication his *A Traveller in Southern Italy* was described as "easily this century's best book [on the region]."

Morton is an excellent travelling companion and I had *A Traveller in Rome* with me every day as I walked the ancient stones of this city. Through him I learned exactly where Julius Caesar had been murdered (not on the Capitol as Shakespeare had it, nor in the Forum as some tour guides tell you, but in the new theatre that Pompey had built about a kilometre away), and that Septimus Sevirus—whose triumphal arch dominates the Forum—was one of the first explorers of the wild and miserable Scotland.

And that one of the two founders of the famous Babington Tea Rooms at the foot of the Spanish Steps was one Miss Isabel Cargill "of Dunedin, New Zealand, whose grandfather was the founder of Otago and whose ancestor was Donald Cargill, the Covenantor".

Here is a typically informative Morton digression as he recounts the history and practices of the vestal Virgins: "A sad tale is revealed. The marble palace was an ice chest in cold weather. It was surrounded by tall temples and built against the side of the Palatine Hill. If you go there in the afternoon, you will see that it is one of the first places to fall into the shadow as the sun passes behind the hill; and it must have done so even earlier when the Palatine was covered in tall palaces.

"In an attempt to fight the cold and damp, the Vestals put in double walls on the side of the hill and raised floors everywhere, sometimes with very oddly sawn-off amphorae. And between these rows of halved wine-jars the hot air was made to circulate from a central furnace. It is melancholy to reflect that honour and sanctity must have been accompanied by rheumatism and arthritis."

Morton's books were long out of circulation—I found my tattered hardback copies in secondhand shops without too much difficulty however—but some (the excellent *A Traveller in Rome* among them) were reprinted a few years ago.

He had fallen into obscurity as a new generation of travel writers headed off to more exotic regions to write about themselves and their responses. Morton rarely indulged in such self-centred frivolity.

His opinion hardly seemed to matter, it was the history in the stones and pathways he was interested in.

And, in almost two dozen refined and crafted books, even now he continues to bring the stones—and statues like that peculiar, overlooked Rienzi piece—to life again.

The Kingfish in his Kingdom

(Louisiana, USA)

✳

THE BULLET HOLES from the shoot-out are still
there. I put my finger in one and look around feeling
the space in this corridor. It is narrow so you can
imagine what the gunplay must have been like: shots
echoing around, one man falling from his wounds and
the other shot dead, the shouting and clack of heels
resonating off the marble floor. . .

Today of course all is quiet, just a few people getting in and out of the hissing lifts or going about their
political business.

But the place in the Louisiana State Capitol Building in Baton Rouge where Dr Carl Weiss shot Huey
Long—known as The Kingfish—still pulls any number
of sightseers, mostly because Long was such a powerful
figure in American life in the Thirties.

Long was an unashamed populist who berated the rich for their greed and wealth, stood up for the little guy, and in 1928 glad-handed his way into the governorship of Louisiana in a landslide victory on the back of his slogan, "Every man a king, but no one wears a crown". Yet when in office he ruled like dictator.

Long was a flamboyant character at a time when poverty and unemployment racked the South: he wore white linen suits; used radio to get his message to the poor folks; and published an autobiography *Every Man A King* in 1933.

Some called him a communist for his social programmes, others said he was a fascist for the way he wielded power in the state.

He might have bad-mouthed the wealthy, but Long also shook their hands and lived among them. His programmes like Share Our Wealth naturally had great appeal during the Depression, and with his quick lawyer's mind he negotiated through legislation that allowed him to appoint all state employees in 1934.

By that time he was a senator in Washington aiming for the White House and had left behind his puppet governor Alvin Olin King.

Long has been celebrated in song, most notably by Randy Newman whose *Good Old Boys* album of 1974 included *Kingfish*: "Who built the highway to Baton Rouge? Who put up the hospital and built you schools? Who looks after shit-kickers like you? The Kingfish do."

On the same album Newman also covered the campaign song that Long co-wrote: "Why weep or slumber

America, land of the brave and true. With castles and clothing and food for all, all belongs to you. Every man a king, every man a king."

These sentiments infuriated Long's enemies and on September 8 1935, while standing in a narrow corridor of the state capitol building in Baton Rouge the Kingfish met his end.

Stories abound as to why Weiss shot Long—and there is a body of evidence to say he didn't, that he only punched Long who was then accidentally cut down by bullets from his own bodyguards while shooting Weiss dead.

Most believe that Weiss was enraged that his father-in-law, a well-known judge, was being levered out of his position by Long. But we'll probably never know, Weiss died on the marble floor.

Long lived a couple of days more—later there were also persistent rumours the doctors had a hand in his death—and legend has it that his final words were, "Don't let me die, I have got so much left to do".

For those who loved him Long never really died: there are bridges and roads all over Louisiana named for him, and there is a statue of him in a quiet garden outside the magnificent Art Deco capitol building which he ordered, the tallest capitol building in the United States.

In a typically grand gesture Long said no building should be constructed to rise higher than this 34-storey monument to himself.

And from the top floor—with the inevitable gift shop today—there is a movingly evocative view of

Long's statue and beyond the Mississippi River where you can see the bridge Long insisted be built so low as to prevent big ships going any further than Baton Rouge.

Up here the Kingfish could truly whisper to himself that he was the king of all he surveyed.

Polo With Pachyderms

(Hua Hin, Thailand)

✳

"THE ENGLISH INVENT the most stupid of sports," says John, and he should know. He's English and we've been talking about cricket.

It is evening and we are sitting at the poolside bar in the sumptuous Anantara Resort and Spa near the coastal town of Hua Hin, three hours by terrifyingly fast taxi south of Bangkok. I arrived yesterday and immediately made for the bar to steady my jangling nerves. That was where I first met John.

The reason for his melancholy outburst tonight is the sport we have spent this September day watching: elephant polo.

You only need to spend a few seconds considering that absurd conjunction of words to be in nodding agreement with the mildly morose John from Exeter.

185

Half an hour down the road at the Somdej Phra Suriyothai military camp, heavily-sponsored teams have battled it out in scorching heat before a tiny audience of corporate guests, a contingent of international media that outnumbers the participants, and a few bemused locals and soldiers who find the few areas of shade available to anyone other than well-heeled guests in corporate tents.

The whole thing has been utterly absurd, but ponderous pachyderms suddenly become as agile as ponies under the guidance of the local mahouts and the players, who carry three metre long sticks and aim for a ball which can often be trampled into the dirt under very large feet.

Yet there is also something oddly enjoyable in this sport where its participants spend as much time being photographed before and after a game as they do banging the ball around. It all feels very quaint and British colonial—and indeed one of the older hands is the handsome Colonel Raj Kalaan from India, known to all as the Silver Fox for his thick white hair.

During the sweaty tournament in tropical heat, plenty of water is drunk, but so are gallons of Chivas Regal thanks to one of the sponsors. And by night these people who play hard party even harder.

Elephant polo is not the sport of the common man: teams are sponsored by heavyweights such as Mercedes Benz, American Express, British Airways and, in the case of the former burly All Blacks from New Zealand (who embarrassingly almost lose to a team of Bangkok transvestites, the hilariously named Screwless

Tuskers), by PricewaterhouseCooper.

This sport isn't for the faint-hearted. Elephants can get up a fair bit of pace and if you've ever been atop one you know it can be a bumpy ride even when they dawdle. Add to that swinging a long stick at a tiny ball, the searing sun, and chukkas (halves) which last well over the allocated seven minutes because of stoppages and you have a game which is... Well, as John says, pretty damn stupid.

But also a lot of fun.

The supporters in the tents—one of which has to-day served a never-ending and ever-changing menu of Chivas cocktails—have bayed with delight as the massive animals galloped around the park followed by a small army of cleaners collecting the small mountains of dung an elephant leaves when in a state of high excitement.

With a cocktail in hand, the Germans sounding like hooray-Henrys, and Torquhil Ian Campbell, the 13th Duke of Argyll in attendance as a player in the Chivas Regal team, this has been a lovely day out in the old colonial manner.

The World Elephant Polo Association which organises this annual event has a long and illustrious history dating back to the days of the British Raj in India. Or so you might expect.

In fact the organisation only established the rules in 1982 and has its headquarters at the Tiger Tops Jungle Lodge in the Royal Chitwan Park in Nepal. It is a registered Olympic sport with the Nepal Olympic Committee.

The rules are similar to horse polo but the field is about a third the size, each team has three elephants, no more than two may be in the D (the area demarked by that pitch marking in front of the goal), and elephants may neither pick up a ball nor lie down in the goalmouth.

And, "sugar cane or rice balls packed with vitamins (molasses and rock salt) shall be given to the elephants at the end of each match and a cold beer or soft drink to the elephant drivers—and not vice versa."

Over the week-long tournament it can be hilariously engaging —I never thought I'd be shouting "elephant in the D" with such fervour, let alone know what it meant. But better is the fact that this curious sport is peopled by larger-than-life characters.

Margie McDougal from Nepal is a fierce and long-time competitor in the Bangkok Bank Ladies team. She haughtily delivered this accidentally ambiguous innuendo to the ladyboys in the Screwless Tuskers after some on-field shenanigans: "If you want to be ladies, play like ladies. No hooking."

The name "Oliver Winter" is heard everywhere, as this skilful player—who imports polo ponies from Germany, Argentina and Brunei—attempts to drive his team to victory yet again.

After a week of heats by day, and parties by night at the Anantara Resort (another high-end sponsor), the Sunday afternoon final was between Australia and Winter's Mercedes Benz Thailand—staged before a huge crowd of tourists, and numerous locals who had heard the hometeam were contenders.

And—in front of a representative of the King who arrived in limo with an entourage—they got the perfect result, the first Thai victory ever.

The English finished well down the rankings, but above the All Blacks.

The King's Cup Elephant Polo Tournament is almost incidentally about elephant polo. It's really about having a very good time.

Peter Prentice of the Chivas team—now two decades an ele-polo player—is a man for whom life is a party. His occasional commentary on the games is punctuated with shameless plugs for the sponsors (and the new pair of Timberlands shoes he bought and was clearly comfortable in), and as the day progresses his hyperbole inflates accordingly.

During the final game he describes the players as "the ultimate athletes" to loud guffaws and applause.

"It's not pretty, but it is elephant polo," he shouts. And when the young Australian team take to the field—after the numerous pre-match photographs which seem obligatory—he bellows, "The whole of Perth, actually the whole of Australia is watching these wonderful young men today."

It adds a farcical and self-deprecating touch to what is otherwise taken very seriously, and is collecting money for a serious cause.

The event raises funds for the Thailand Elephant Conservation Centre in Lampang, northern Thailand—which provides welfare, sustenance, medical care and employment for the Kingdom's 1500 wild and 2500 domesticated elephants. To date it has raised around

US$85,000 and people are prepared to dig deep in their pockets, especially at the Saturday night auction which comes after another long dinner at Anantara and plenty of drinks.

Up for auction are return flights to the UK on British Airways (another sponsor), mobile phones (from another, Mobile Easy Thailand) and paintings by elephants. All of them realise bids well beyond their market value—although it is admittedly hard to assess the value of a painting by an elephant. Over US$200 as it turns out.

When the first elephant polo tournament was launched in Thailand there were only six teams participating. Now there are 14 and a waiting list. This competition in a bizarre "sport" is the sixth largest event on the Thai tourism calendar and gets international coverage, because so many media parasites such as myself are flown in to be entertained, wined and dined. None of us carrying gifts from Chivas Regal will go home unhappy—except maybe my drinking buddy John.

On the final night John and I are, inevitably, back in the cool poolside bar in the Anantara. We are laughing about the absurdity of this game which has obviously been invented by rich people with too much time on their hands. But we are also agreeing just how enjoyable these few days have been.

"You were right the other night," I say cheerily. "It's a bloody stupid sport, but a lot of fun. Especially the post-match parties."

"Yes, we invent stupid sports," he says turning

glum again. "Then everyone beats us at them."

Don't Forget to Remember

(Texas, USA)

�֍

ON A HOT, DRY Monday morning I'm sitting outside of what remains of the old Alamo in the centre of
San Antonio, Texas. From here the Crockett Hotel—
built in the 1850s and renovated many times since—
looms above the historic mission, and street cars and
taxis rumble across land which was once splattered
with the blood of hundreds.

Tourists, few of them international if the visitors
book can be believed, are starting to waddle through
the old barracks where the worst of the carnage took
place.

"If y'all ask me," says the portly Texan beside me,
"they never had a chance anyways. Them walls he'ya
is far too low."

We look at the low collection of brick and stone.
He's right. The battle for the Alamo was a forgone

conclusion, so any retelling of the story—and there are many variants—isn't one of military strategy. It is of the inevitability of a massacre.

And that's why it's a legend.

Most people my age remember the Alamo. That was where John Wayne, Captain Travis and Jim Bowie (pronounced "Boo-ee" and of some kind of knife fame) fought off hordes of pesky Mexicans wearing tight trousers and boasting evil moustaches.

After that I don't remember much except that Wayne (as Davy Crockett, who gave his name to the nearby hotel and a mini-golf course in his home state of Tennessee which I passed a week ago) died valiantly and the name of the Alamo lives forever as a defining moment of heroism in American folklore.

From our cultural distance the Alamo—as in the ringing if somewhat empty phrase "Remember the Alamo"—doesn't mean much. But it has infected popular culture.

The basement of the Alamo is where Pee Wee Herman headed to find his missing bike in *Pee Wee's Big Adventure*, for example.

Oddly enough, Davy Crockett has always meant something special to me: in my family the lore is that when I was about five I sang *The Ballad of Davy Crockett* loudly at the top of the Eiffel Tower—and the 78 RPM record of that song by Rusty Draper (flip side, *Lazy Mule*) was the first record I ever owned.

Like Scrooge McDuck who kept his first dime, I still have my copy of Draper's upbeat ballad on the Mercury Playcraft label—which came in a paper sleeve with what looks like a pencil drawing of the impossibly handsome Fess Parker on the cover. Parker played Crockett in the famous Disney movie when I was an impressionable and impromptu singer—and later he was also Daniel Boone, in the long-running 60s television serial.

The distinctively red-haired Draper, whose name is barely known these days and is rarely acknowledged as having sung *The Ballad of Davy Crockett*, sold a whopping 30 million records in his long career, and only died in 2003 at age 80.

Sitting in the sun on this clear day I am scrolling the lyrics in my head ("born on a mountain top in Tennessee, greenest state in the land of the free") and also remembering a less tuneful song by Donovan in the 60s: "A hunnid'n'eighty were challenged by Travis to die, by a line that he drew with sword when the battle was nigh".

I am dragging up Crockett and Alamo references.

At the start of some dissolute 70s tour the Rolling Stones posed here looking like drug-addled buccaneers. Quite why the place and pose was never clear to me.

Oh, and Ozzy Osbourne back in the good old days when he was drinking earned the ire of San Antonians. His wife Sharon hid his clothes one night so he couldn't go out, but Ozzy put on one of her dresses and headed for the nearest bar. But he got caught short on the way back so urinated on an old brick wall. It was, unfortunately for him, the historic Alamo.

These are perhaps not the things you are expected to call to mind when asked to "Remember the Alamo".

The more recent Billy Bob Thornton movie *The Alamo*—in which Thornton plays a convincing and engaging Crockett owing nothing to the downhome wise-cracking and tight-lipped heroics of John Wayne—gave the story of the siege by Santa Anna's Mexican army in 1836 a chance to breathe free of some of the more shallow cultural accretions it has acquired.

The myths surrounding the Alamo, like those of the British at Dunkirk, is one of military failure turned into moral victory.

In short, a ragtag band of about 180 Texians (as they were then called) holed up in the old mission station and faced down Santa Anna's army of a few thousand for 13 days. They expected and waited for relief that didn't come. Travis' famous letter to other revolutionaries to come and assist them said, "victory or death".

It was never going to be the former, and they all knew it.

Call it heroism or call it folly (it was certainly a measure of both), the actions of those men inside the walls who knew they were going to die has been distilled into the spirit of Texas. It's less commonly known, however, that they weren't there to fight for America against Mexico, but for the independent Republic of Texas (which lasted almost a decade before Texas became a state).

All this—and the bickering between Travis and the boozy, sick Bowie, the aftermath when that catch-phrase was on the lips of their avengers, and the defeat of Santa Anna who was a treaty-breaking dictator and self-styled "Napoleon of the West"—is in the Billy Bob movie. But neither that nor the Imax version around the corner from the old mission prepares you for the actual battle site itself.

The remaining Alamo buildings—much like Elvis' Graceland—are surprisingly small. Their mythic stature has inflated them in the popular imagination.

The whole Alamo site no longer exists of course; progress took care of that. What remains is the old mission (no, there's no basement so Pee Wee's bike couldn't have been there) and the long barrack which is now a museum. The old outer wall and compound are long gone. But they were just that, a low wall and a big empty bit the size of a football field.

When Santa Anna's troops scaled that outer wall in the early hours of March 6 after almost a fortnight of assault and attrition the rest was just a slaughter. They easily vaulted the lower inner wall and the barracks became a blood-splattered charnel house as the Mexicans, ordered to kill everyone, fought their way by bayonet, musket and knife through the narrow corridor.

It's an eerie thought so many men died here brutally where tourists now walk chatting on cellphones and sucking water bottles.

But the museum in the barracks doesn't shy away from uncomfortable truths about the Alamo, notably that Travis might just have been a wrongheaded, arrogant cuss for a start.

He had abandoned his wife and children (which is in the current movie but not in many other versions) and was only 26. The famous Jim Bowie who died on his bed with pistol in hand was an equally flawed "hero". He had made his fortune in slave-smuggling with the Gulf Coast pirate Jean Lafitte. And it wasn't Jim who gave his name to that knife but his brother Rezin, a real nasty bastard according to contemporary accounts.

Of the defenders, very few were professional soldiers. Among their ranks were doctors, lawyers, settlers, opportunists and Micajah Autry from North Carolina whose occupation was listed as "poet".

Crockett is the most interesting figure. A fiddle-playing, former senator from Tennessee, he had been rejected by his constituency the previous year. According to what this reluctant hero and storyteller told his gathered comrades in the Alamo, he had left his ungrateful voters with the ringing phrase: "They might all go to Hell, and I would go to Texas."

For him Hell and Texas turned out to be the same place.

The Billy Bob film, which controversially follows a Mexican soldier's version of events, shows Crockett captured and executed. Traditionalists have cried foul and that heroic David (as he was always known in life) would never have allowed himself to be taken.

He isn't in the John Wayne or Imax versions.

The story of the defence of the Alamo is one of foolishness, idealism, heroism, politics and a massacre. And the old stone building—just above the romantic Riverwalk in San Antonio with its Tex-Mex restaurants, galleries, Hard Rock Cafe and sports bars—attracts tens of thousands every day in summer. Locals

will, unprompted, tell you it is one of the most popular
tourist sites in the country.

The Alamo is where legend, tragedy, blood and a
fighting spirit were melded in the crucible of history.

Separating the myth and merchandising from the
actual story with all its nuances and nasty politics can
be difficult. But it is worth the effort to sit quietly and
try to assimilate it all.

Or you can simply go to the gift shop and buy a
ballpoint pen shaped like Crockett's long rifle, a coon-
skin Crockett cap, some of the dozens of Alamo caps
and t-shirts, the tie with the Texas flag on it, the fridge-
magnet Alamo thermometer, the dress-up Davy doll...

Remember the Alamo?

My God, there are San Antonio folk determined
Americans not only never forget, but buy up bags of
merchandising detritus and make the Alamo a mundane part of their everyday lives.

That might be the greatest defeat of all.

Hill, in a High Place

(Washington State, USA)

⁂

SAM HILL HAD a vision fairly common among the wealthy: an agrarian utopia where happy workers would toil in fertile fields, their cheery lives overseen by their benign master—himself, of course—from a bastion high on a hill above.

Unfortunately Sam—a railway man and an incurable builder of roads—picked the wrong hill in the wrong place. It is near The Dalles in north central Oregon, a crossroad city we ended up in on our way to Seattle.

The Dalles was given its unusual name by French-Canadian trappers. It means gutter stones and the place is so called because the trappers saw the towering rocky bluffs channelling the nearby Columbia River in much the same manner. The riverside settlement was the end of the Oregon Trail and from here for-

tune seekers would take the Columbia 300 winding kilometres to the Pacific coast, or make for the productive Willamette Valley overland about 150 kilometres
southwest.

All fascinating historical stuff to be sure, and bold
murals on brick buildings in the old part of the town
depict famous moments in the life of The Dalles. But
there seemed no pressing reason to linger here until,
over breakfast, Chuck (owner of the Windrider Inn
where we have spent the night) mentions Sam Hill.

"Man, you gotta go see his place," he laughs. "It's
enormous. And while you're up there check out his
Stonehenge down the road."

This sounds too crazy to ignore so after coffee and
handshakes we drive back east along the Columbia and
cross into Washington state where Hill purchased 6000
acres of land in 1907.

His vision was of a Quaker farming community
working riverside land where the moderate climate ensured that fruit ripened and crops grown here would
mature a few weeks before those in other parts of the
state.

It was, at least in his imaginings, the ideal place for
his own personal utopia. The view wasn't bad either.

So Hill ordered the building of a palatial home—
Maryhill, named for his daughter—on the windblown
bluff above with a view of the farmland and mighty
Columbia below, and what appears to be half of Oregon
on the opposite side.

"I expect this house to be here for a thousand years
after I am gone," Hill grandly announced when con-

struction on the three-storey building began in 1914. Unfortunately not many others wanted to live in this remote place.

You can imagine their question: "The Dalles? And where would that be?"

Within a few years it was obvious Hill's utopia would never be realised. Work at Maryhill ceased.

But that's where the story of Maryhill really begins.

Hill travelled widely and in Europe had made friends with the avant-garde dancer and choreographer Marie Louise Fuller. When she heard of the building standing incomplete she suggested Hill finish it and turn the place into an art museum.

The idea appealed to Hill. After all, what else was he going to do with it?

In 1926 Maryhill was dedicated by his friend, Queen Marie of Romania who donated her wedding dress and heavy, somewhat ugly, wooden furniture from her castles out of gratitude for the assistance Hill had given in the reconstruction of her country after World War I.

But that's not all that is in this breeze-battered but absorbing museum.

A middle-aged docent points us towards the utterly unexpected here in the most empty part of Washington: a large permanent exhibition of Rodin sculpture, drawings and plaster models; and the section devoted to the extraordinary life of Fuller.

Born near Chicago in 1862 Fuller had, by her late twenties, appeared in theatrical productions and Buffalo Bill's travelling show, and performed at London's Gaiety Theatre where she observed dancers using flowing skirts to create a sense of free-flowing movement.

She learned the visual power of coloured lighting on gossamer silk and long swathes of the material, and adapted the Gaiety style to create what she called her Serpentine Dance. She performed this to audiences in America but felt she wasn't being fully appreciated for the innovator she undoubtedly was. In 1892, however, she performed it at the Folies Bergere in Paris, was an overnight sensation, and became a symbol of the Belle Epoque era. She was, according to later writers, the embodiment of the Art Nouveau movement and her company presented Isadora Duncan to enthusiastic Parisians.

Fuller's most famous piece was a dance to Debussy's *La Mer* in which waves of shimmering silk were moved by dancers beneath her costume.

Fuller, known as La Loie and who enjoyed a number of lesbian relationships, enhanced her performances with lantern slides, coloured gels and florescent paint, and had a laboratory built in her studio where she could experiment with colour. She consulted Thomas Edison on the use of light, and the Curies about their work in electricity and with radium.

The writer Stephane Mallarme hailed her performances as "an artistic intoxication and an industrial achievement".

At Maryhill there is jerky footage of one of her many imitators and even that, capturing the sensuous flow of layered silk and other diaphanous fabrics, is thrilling.

Her friend Auguste Rodin—whose work she

collected—considered her "a woman of genius". Anatole France—the French writer and critic who won the Nobel Prize for Literature in 1921—wrote the introduction to her autobiography, and she counted among her devoted following Jean Cocteau.

Fuller died in Paris in 1928 and is buried in Pere Lachaise: "A magician is dead, a butterfly has folded its wings" said one French newspaper.

But Maryhill, to which she donated her Rodin collection, is as much her legacy as it is that of moneyman and patron Hill.

Downstairs in a huge airy gallery are the Rodin drawings and sculpture (including models and studies for his greatest works like *Balzac* and *The Burghers of Calais*), and period photographs and posters of Fuller.

But within Hill's eclectic collection there is also a section devoted to Native American cultures along the Columbia, and a changing display of exotic chess sets which include some from Cambodia, Indonesia (the pieces as characters from the Ramayana), India (in Mogul style with a male counsellor rather than a queen) and China.

"Not many people outside the state know about us," says our prim docent as we are admiring the chess pieces. "I think that's quite a pity, don't you?"

We nod in mute agreement. You don't see a queen's wedding dress the size of a small car every day, least of all in the Pacific Northwest.

Down one of Hill's roads is his full-scale concrete replica of Stonehenge, built as tribute to soldiers of the county who lost their lives in World War I.

But it is not a war memorial. Hill was told, incorrectly, that the original Stonehenge had been a place of sacrifice. His replica was built to remind people that humanity was still being sacrificed to the god of war.

Standing here, the wind whipping straight down from Canada, it is hard to imagine what drew Sam Hill—who died in 1931 and is buried on the hill below—to this lofty and lonely bluff.

But he was an uncommon man: a Quaker pacifist during the turbulent war years; a man who made his money in heavy industry but harboured the dream of a farming community; and a patron of the quiet arts who took great joy and excitement from noisy railways and roads.

We walk back to Sam's monumental museum, nod hello to the only other two people here on this day, and sign the visitors' book.

The docent glides up and looks at what we have written.

"New Zealand? And where would that be?"

Woke Up, it was a Chelsea Morning

(New York City, USA)

✳

STANLEY LIKED TO talk but, to be fair, he had a lot to talk about. Stanley—portly, smiling, intense—was the manager at New York's famous, notorious even, Chelsea Hotel at 222 West 23rd St, his historic home and legendary legacy most recently sold out from under him.

Stanley had inherited the position from his father David Bard who bought it in 1940, and Stanley had grown up in the corridors of this building which was the tallest in Manhattan when it opened in 1884. Back then it has been at the centre of the theatre district. Sarah Bernhardt loved the place.

It had originally been 100 apartments but most of them had subsequently been split into smaller rooms and suites.

The Chelsea—which was declared a New York landmark building in 1966—always had many permanent residents. Stanley told me of the painter Alphaeus Cole who lived there for 35 years until he died at 112.

The composer and critic Virgil Thompson stayed even longer, 54 years.

The list of famous residents and guests is long: Mark Twain, Thomas Wolfe, the boozers Brendan Behan and Dylan Thomas; Patti Smith with Robert Mapplethorpe; William Burroughs who wrote *The Naked Lunch* here; Stanley Kubrick would come to see author Arthur C. Clarke who was here working on the screenplay for *2001: A Space Odyssey*; poet Allen Ginsberg, Bob Dylan, and Warhol's crowd in the 60s...

Janis Joplin famously had sex with Leonard Cohen here (Leonard sang about it in *Chelsea Hotel #2*) and Chelsea Clinton is sort of named after the place. More correctly, she's named after the song *Chelsea Morning* which Joni Mitchell wrote about the hotel.

Jimi Hendrix was once mistaken for a bellboy as he waited in the lobby, and Sid Vicious killed his girlfriend Nancy Spungen in a room upstairs. You can't rent it although many try to, it has since been converted into an apartment.

I'd stayed a few nights in a front room beneath the famous sign. The television picked up only static, the bedside lamps didn't work and the bathroom was clean although the water flow was barely serviceable. But it was an experience.

Sometimes I would just sit in the lobby and look at the art which had been given as payment in lieu of rent

by the likes of Larry Rivers. (The Jackson Pollock has
long gone, to Stanley's place some whisper.)

Every day there was a parade of the famous, the
near-famous or the barely breathing who would make
their way to the rickety elevator by the desk. One day
some people set up for a Mariah Carey video shoot
which took all day and Mariah didn't show. Two films
a year are shot in the corridors and rooms, $9\frac{1}{2}$ *Weeks*
among them.

On my final morning after paying the reasonable
bill I asked if it was possible to meet the manager,
explaining that I was a journalist.

"Don't worry about it, Stanley always likes to talk
to journalists," said the middle-aged man who I had
observed dispensing keys and wisdom to guests.

And so I sat in Stanley's front office which was a
landslide of papers, letters, accounts and old newspapers. He indicated an untidily stacked and overcrowded
bookcase.

"All of those books were written here at the
Chelsea," he said.

He didn't rate the one by the self-confessed "bad
pornographic novelist" Florence Turner who lived here
for a decade until 1975 and wrote about the residents.
Maybe that was because she suggested Stanley was
tight with money.

He told me of the hippies who took over the place in
the 60s, how Sid Vicious was very polite, that residents
keep to themselves, and of how each room has its own
character.

"Every room here is different," he said. "Lemme

show you."

Stanley lead me through the long and tatty corridors on the third floor and opened a door.

"Here's the room Angela Bowie just stayed in," he said gesturing around a spacious suite where the former Mrs David had luxuriated. Another smaller room had an unexpected view over what appeared to be a private garden.

Finally he took me to the room he had decorated himself and was saving until last so I could enjoy the full effect. He paused at the door as if to prepare himself for an unveiling.

Then he dramatically pushed it open to reveal a migraine in the making: the table and bedhead were designed like a snail's shell, there was a mirror the same shape, spirals were on the carpets and a wall-hanging. It was utterly mad.

"I call it the Snail Room," said Stanley with a beam of pride.

I must have been two blocks away before I realised I was still laughing.

Of Queen and Country

(Tennessee, USA)

�֎

THE UGLIEST BABY I ever saw—a pug-faced killer-midget with malevolent eyes—was at Loretta Lynn's place.

Then again, there was plenty of ugly, kitschy, evil and just plain tacky stuff at the home of this country music legend.

But I'll be forgiving, and say that maybe the baby just looked bad in comparison with the delightful setting of Hurricane Mills, the property Loretta bought in the late 60s and which included a working mill beside a pretty lake, and rolling fields in the lush landscapes of east Tennessee about an hour from the capital of country music, Nashville.

We had been driving to Nashville on Interstate 40 when a sign loomed up on the highway ahead: Loretta Lynn Dude Ranch.

Not having read her autobiography *Coal Miner's Daughter*—or having seen the 1980 film adaptation in which Sissy Spacek played Lynn and Tommy Lee Jones was Lynn's husband Doolittle—I had no idea Loretta had a ranch open to the public. But the thought of it is too good to miss, so we pull off the highway and drive to a restaurant-cum-gift shop on a hill above the side road where Loretta's name was bannered large above the entrance.

Lynn—who made her name with appealingly earthy and honest songs like *Don't Come Home A Drinkin' (With Lovin' On Your Mind)*, *The Other Woman*, and *Who's Gonna Take The Garbage Out*—is a country star of the old kind. Her story of rags-to-riches has been told in her autobiographical songs and two volumes of her life story (*Coal Miner's Daughter* and the repetitive sequel *Still Woman Enough*).

She sang of cheatin' husbands, bein' poor but still havin' dignity, of belief in God when the world has done you wrong, and of lost love. Loretta knew all these things from bitter experience.

While buying jars of her jam and a recipe book of downhome cooking (Coca Cola Cake and You Ain't Woman Enough Casserole included) to amuse the folks back home, the young girl behind the counter says Lynn's home is "just down the road apiece, if y'all is innerested".

That was the dude ranch, this was just the merchandise store.

We drive through fragrant countryside lined with wildflowers, cross Duck River (where Loretta's son Jack drowned in 1984) and the road narrows to almost a single lane through a silent forest. Down a broad driveway on our left is Hurricane Mills, a small town of the original post office, a few other buildings and the mill and wheel beside a flat pond.

It is as purty as a picture and facing it across the river is the white columned house which Loretta and Doo moved into in early 1967.

In *Coal Miner's Daughter*—which reads less like a biography than rambling but informative transcripts of conversations with her co-author—Lynn says when she first saw the three storeyed ante-bellum mansion she thought it was like Tara in the movie *Gone With The Wind.*

"It looked like a hillbilly's dream."

Loretta—and Doo, who died in 1996—moved out in the late 70s after fans just kept turning up to the door (and some tempting boozy Doo off for drinks). But the house has been kept as it was when they lived there.

And it's tacky.

Lynn's early life was unashamedly tough and she has written and sung about how she grew up in remote Butcher Holler in Kentucky. She went to a one-room school; their single-room handmade cabin was wallpapered with pages from magazines; she wore flour sacks as a child and slept on the floor until she was nine; and her father worked in the mine.

On the day of her wedding in the local courthouse she needed to go to the toilet so Doo took her to the bus station. She'd never seen indoor plumbing and was terrified by the flushing.

Doo called her a stupid hillbilly—and Lynn admits she was. But forgive her, she was young.

Loretta married Doo when she was 14—he was in his 20s and had fought in Europe in World War II—and had no idea how babies were made. She had four by the time she was 18.

What separates Lynn from many other successful country artists is she genuinely hasn't changed her attitudes: she doesn't know big words and doesn't pretend to; and admits to some hilarious gaffes.

When she was invited to a Dean Martin Celebrity Roast for Jack Lemmon she didn't have any lunch that day. She was looking forward to the roast meat and potatoes later.

Ernest Tubb, the country legend who helped her career in the early 60s, said she was the only person he'd met—and through the Grand Ole Opry he'd met 'em all—who didn't change after she became famous.

Lynn has known six presidents and in *Still Woman Enough* she says she counted two of 'em as friends, Jimmy Carter and the first George Bush. Of course she supported George the Younger.

Yet while she has mixed with the great and the good—and the not-so-good—she also remembered what being poor felt like and so wasted nothing.

She kept the packaging that perfume bottles came in and at Hurricane Mills there is a museum filled with her dresses, concert posters, memorabilia and her old tour bus.

Shortly after Doo first met Loretta he gave her a

baby doll for Christmas and said that when they were married they would have a real live doll.

"I didn't know what he was talking about," she later said.

But, like most things in her life, she kept that gift. The child-bride was, after all, still playing with dolls.

Over the years as she became wealthy they added to Hurricane Mills.

She built a replica of the house she grew up in on a hill above the town so her fans could see what her early life had been like. Although slightly larger than the original it is full of detail like the magazine and newspaper wallpaper, and it has a tiny kitchen and outhouse.

The day we dropped by there were a dozen other visitors to Hurricane Mills, among them a couple who—and I dislike myself for making this observation—could have been siblings and had two slightly unusual looking children with them.

The man was ill-shaven and wore ragged denim overalls, and the woman a baggy hand-me-down dress. They tip-toed around Loretta's house and gazed in awe at the hideously carved Indian kitsch on the walls (Loretta was proud of her Cherokee heritage) and the cabinets Doo built to house her collection of salt and pepper shakers and such like.

They became reverently silent at the sight of her gold and platinum discs in the stairwell, and in the garden took dozens of photos of the hideous job-lot statuary.

These people—worshippers in the church of

country—were Loretta's true fans and the people who gave her the career she has had. And she never forgot it.

Hurricane Mills has trail rides, camping grounds, fishing holes, regular concerts and an annual Motor-Cross Championship. Loretta's constituency turns up in their thousands during the year and make the pilgrimage to her house like others visit the Vatican or Buckingham Palace.

"Horses down that away" reads a sign.

I could only be cynical at the reconstruction of the mine her daddy worked in—it was kinda dark and scary in there though—but was impressed by the ebb and flow of her career as outlined in the massive museum of her memorabilia.

Lynn recently released an album with Jack White of the White Stripes, and so Loretta—at 69—was a cool name to drop among the hip set. People who'd previously never heard a note she'd sung suddenly confessed to being longtime closet fans.

In a reminder of what a footnote in her long career that association had been, two posters of concerts with White were stacked in a corner near the toilets.

But she had kept them, just as she kept and displayed the gifts from fans.

Beside the shop was her doll museum.

That is where I saw the brutally ugly baby, in a glass case beside the Native American dolls, those in chintzy wedding gowns, or dressed as cowgirls in gingham. Awful stuff, all of it.

The ugly baby was on its hands and knees, it's

oddly distorted face twisted up into something between a snarl, a grimace and a plea for help. It's pinched eyes were almost Satanic and, most curious of all, its nappies were pulled down to reveal a round firm bottom raised in the air.

It looked... well, creepy actually. And not a little perverted.

I'm sure that other couple and their kids will never forget the day they went to Loretta Lynn's place.

Nor will I.

But for entirely different reasons.

And the Dream Goes On

(Queenstown, New Zealand)

�֎

NINE MONTHS AGO my life wasn't like this. Everything was different.

Then, the hard white sun would melt the early morning cool and the air would thicken with the smell of decaying jungle vegetation. On the cracked pavement of the town's only main street, women would squat in doorways avoiding the equatorial heat as they sold their meagre produce.

Men walked aimlessly in the alleys, and in the market would fill their empty days by gambling for tiny sums.

A rusting steamer at the wharf attracted a curious few, so did a sick dog beside a pile of rubbish in a sun-bleached backstreet.

Some days there would be no water, most days the power would go off. In my fetid, cheap motel room—

the mattress covered by two worn sheets and what looked like an old tablecloth—the air would solidify and I'd be gasping for breath. The brown fungal walls sweated.

At dusk people in the dusty town would rake rubbish into piles and set them alight. The humid air filled with a smoky haze and the acrid stench of burning plastic. Ash would drift in shades of grey across the blue sky. It blurred the horizon beyond the palm trees where the ocean, often a shimmering azure by day, would gradually seep into the impenetrable black of darkness.

And then there might be gunshots.

But that was nine months ago, and in a necklace of tropical islands in the West Pacific which were sliding into the endless night of uncertainty and random violence.

For two weeks—with photographer Alan Gibson—I endured the heat and dust of Honiara, the capital of the Solomon Islands. Then we returned home, for me to write of conversations with broken men on broken streets.

I tried to tell of the debilitating corruption, and what the end of hope can feel like. Of young men who looked at the horizon every day and wondered what might lie beyond. It was a world of failed dreams, and worse.

It was a place where dreaming had ceased.

The irony is that what I wrote about there has brought me here, to this place where everything is different.

My partner and I are now by the lake in impossibly picturesque Queenstown in New Zealand's South Island. The nearby hills have an icing-sugar dust of snow on their smooth sides. Beyond, black mountains rise to razor-edged whitened points which pierce the low cloud. Tourists with albatross-like cameras around their necks and brand-heavy trainers walk the lakeside. They fill the restaurants with careless laughter. Rooms are warmed by friendships, relaxation runs through the town like an epidemic.

Outside it is cold, the air clear. This is a safe world, for us one of comfort and pampering.

These new days are saturated in that disconcerting irony: my reward for writing well about the poverty, gun culture and dazed lives of people in the Solomons is a complimentary weekend in one of the Small Luxury Hotels of the World, the up-market Eichardt's on the shore of Lake Wakatipu.

This, my partner says, is the physics of feature writing: for every story there is an equal and opposite story.

From the balcony of our room—or more correctly rooms—we have a view across the motionless lake.

A possum-fur rug is thrown across a bed the size of an aircraft carrier, and our private lounge has an open fire. There is a CD selection available, complimentary cocktails before dinner, and a dozen channels on the television.

The decor in these renovated rooms in the historic white building on Marine Parade is a subtle blend of beige and pale chocolate. There is real art on the walls, antiques in the hallway, and recessed floor-level lighting comes on in the large bathroom at night.

Eichardt's was built brick-by-brick in 1866, served time as a tavern and boarding house, then was extensively renovated in 2001 as one of the few exclusive luxury hotels in the country. It has been winning awards ever since.

A couple of television types have been recent guests in one the five suites, so have top people from *The Financial Times* and *Forbes*, and any number of writers for high-end travel magazines and tourism companies.

At something like $1200 a night, the luxury life probably doesn't come much more luxurious.

Everything here feels soft and inviting. Deserved even.

On the first afternoon I stretch out on the recliner with a drink from the minibar and watch the news.

And there it is. That tragic country.

One brief image and I am back there, the layers of luxury dropping away. I am mesmerised. The journalist is standing on a street I recognise and talking of New Zealand soldiers who have come to put order into this chaotic land.

There's a gung-ho quality about the broadcast which I find transparent. It suggests the endgame, a redemption at hand, a complex situation distilled to comforting soundbites. I have no doubt what is being said is true, a lot of things about the Solomons are. Especially the lies.

In the midst of comfort I have a feeling of unease, like something is about to happen. I scan the channels to see if there is more.

The following morning Queenstown yawns and stretches under a cloudless sky. We drive around the mountain and point a camera at high peaks with each other in the foreground. We run into thick mud on the way to a place called Paradise. So we spin the rental around, turn up the heater and head along another slushy road between the towering peaks. We drive past farms of delicate deer and huge cattle, and stop to admire a handsome 10-point stag which watches us nervously from behind the wire fencing.

As the sun slides behind the mountain range the air starts to bite. On the drive back to the open fire in our sumptuous hotel I am somewhere in the Solomons again: thinking of the generous people I met on the island of Malaita; of the crazy man released from the asylum because there was no one to look after it anymore; of being invited to a wedding feast in a small village; of kids playing with the balloons I would give them.

And of White River, a scrappy market of half a dozen tables where women sell betel nut, bananas and coconuts to no one. It is only 10 minutes out of Honiara, but is the limit of safe passage. I remember young guys with hooded eyes beneath their blood red bandannas surrounding me and accepting the offer of cigarettes in menacing, sullen silence.

Nosing the car into the lakeside parking lot under an empty sky I feel uneasy again.

The following day we drive to Glenorchy and the start of the Routeburn Track where vivid moss is soaked by a steady cold rain. We breathe deep in chilly air, watch as a hawk circles silently beneath low-slung clouds. And so our day goes by: still, quiet, safe.

That night, walking after dinner beneath the invisible peaks, there is an endless black canopy above spotted with stars. Couples stroll glove-in-glove, the night feels secure and silent. In our room is a complementary bottle of port, vintage cheeses, dried figs and apricots, and paper thin crackers laid out on the bedside table.

I open the port and watch the late news. And I am taken back again.

Stories of refugees from the Weathercoast where mad Harold Keke has been on a killing spree. I am remembering: the bullet holes in the car; the taxi driver and his drunken, armed passenger; the afternoon laughing teenage soldiers headed off to the Weathercoast in a small boat, drinking beer. Some never returned.

That night as I am drifting into sleep there is laughter from the street below. A woman is saying something I cannot decipher through my drowsiness. I drag her into my dream. She is shouting now, the truck has overturned and I am aware of the shooting.

I am at White River. There is gunfire around me, the woman is screaming, children are huddled wide-eyed beneath the broken tables in the mud and the rebel boys are shooting at nothing in particular. I run across the road as bullets crack into the white walls of the bridge. Coins of concrete fly through the air. A convoy rumbles through.

I slide down the bank to the river and scramble

under the bridge. An unknown man I have seen before is there, he puts his fingers to his lips to silence me then moves off, disappearing down the rocky riverbed. I climb up the other side and am in a house of dark rooms filled with trees. A woman is standing in a doorway surrounded by flames. A siren is screaming.

I wake with a start and above the silent streets of Queenstown is the wail of the volunteer fire-brigade siren.

I slide out of bed, my feet on the warm possum-fur rug which has fallen to the floor, and walk to the bathroom with its gleaming mirrors and bottles of body lotion.

I wash my face and take a glass of water. My hands are shaking.

And I am in one of the small luxury hotels of the world.

That afternoon we are winging our way above the blue marble lake. It looks unnaturally silent.

This world is secure and reassuring. There are no surprises here, no sudden movement in the bushes, no unfamiliar sounds by night. The strands of cloud move slow, the air is clean, the watery sun brings a gentle warmth.

Down there are tidy townships where there is power and water and predictability.

And a place called Paradise.

These are very different days.

The following morning I am back at work. That afternoon in the office there is talk of me returning to the Solomons.

PART III

The Idiot Boy Who Flew

A strange journey begins with some good advice—the saint and storyteller—from Amalfi to ugly—the romance of Italy considered—a shocking discovery—the sad south—the idiot boy—the flying men of a faraway place—even more aerial saints—the hometown of the idiot boy—inflationary practices among the Catholics—once upon a time of miracles—the why and wherefore—a dark drive and a wisdom revealed.

�֎

GIUSEPPE'S BIRD-NEST EYEBROWS appear above the top of his newspaper. I have told him I am hiring a car and, nervously, am about to drive in Italy for the first time. He considers me in silence then patiently puts the paper down and offers some advice. "Just ignore everyone else," he says with a laconic shrug of indifference and downturn of his mouth. "That is all. So, you just carry on and ignore everything that is all around you, and do it for yourself."

225

He looks at me over his spectacles for a moment more then returns to his reading.

This is probably an excellent injunction, but here in Sorrento the streets can be impossibly narrow and wing mirrors invite collateral damage. Cars, motorcycles, trucks and vans argue for space with slow walking locals and the few inattentive tourists still drifting around at the end of the summer season.

And then there is the journey ahead: just the first few hours from here through Positano and down the Amalfi Coast are fraught with dangers. Two days previous I had taken a bus to picturesque Positano on a road where barely 50 metres is straight and the route hugs the cliff the whole way. A moment's inattention and we would have been cast onto the rocks hundreds of metres below.

On the return trip I'd noticed the driver—who regularly sounded his horn on the hairpin bends—crossed himself a couple of times before particularly sharp, blind corners. This was not encouraging.

At the hire car company the eye-catching, self-consciously aloof girl with heavy kohl eyeliner and immaculately manicured nails is equally indifferent to my qualms as she hands me the keys, documents and a map of the streets of Sorrento. Our trip will take in the Amalfi Coast and back roads through villages in the south, then motorways where cars pass at 200kph, and eventually up to the chaos that is Naples. I take out every piece of insurance offered.

The only vehicle we can afford is a manual so I cautiously negotiate the way back to our hotel noting one advantage of a car is we don't have to deal with the gritty and gummy dog shit on these otherwise orderly and attractive tree-lined side streets.

My wife Megan and I pick up our bags, farewell a bemused Giuseppe, and I point the bonnet towards the narrow and easily-missed turnoff to Positano. I miss it easily and so circle back, trying to ignore everyone who is beeping or making gestures of frustration because I keep hitting the wipers instead of the indicator.

I make the loop to the turnoff and we are on our way, along the winding road across the high mountainous peninsula to where picturesque villages and towns seem to grow up the hillsides.

By chance we have started in the early afternoon when many people have shut up shop and got off the road, so there are fortunately few cars to ignore on this serpentine road. Laughably, every now and again, signs warn of sharp curves for the next few kilometres.

After a while I manage to enjoy the smell of orange groves, the whitewashed houses clinging to cliffs, the view of the shimmering, turquoise Mediterranean beneath us.

This may be a challenging drive along a narrow road, but it is also an appealing one—and the locals know it. We stop for fruit, cheeses and something to drink at a colourful barrow on a small lay-by above a sharp precipice. It is a blaze of fresh oranges, green beans and cucumbers, bright red peppers and yellow lemons. The sign says in English: "Photo free with purchase".

Before us are the white houses and hotels of Positano and the ceramic dome of the seaside church.

By Amalfi the driving has become effortless and I feel our journey to the town of Copertino in the southern region of Puglia has begun.

Copertino—which makes it into few maps and is halfway down the heel of the boot—has an extraordinary claim to fame.

A little over 400 years ago Giuseppe Desa—canonised in 1767 —was born here.

And he flew.

*   *   *

The story of a flying saint came to me by chance. A week before going to Europe I was flicking the pages of Norman Douglas' 1915 travel book *Old Calabria*. Douglas had also chanced on the story of St Joseph, as he called him.

He tells of being in a bookshop in Naples and seeing an 18th century engraving in the front of a volume "which depicted a man raised above the ground without any visible means of support—flying, in short".

Intrigued by this image and on being told it was Joseph of Copertino, Douglas bought that biography, and others, of this "seventeenth century pioneer of aviation".

From his readings Douglas learned various stories of this saint, including that he would occasionally take passengers with him on spontaneous levitations.

The absurdity of these stories is amusing: there is one about Joseph tossing a sheep in the air, flying up to catch it then hovering at tree height for two hours; "his outdoor record", quips Douglas.

But Douglas also appears to vouch for the veracity of some of these aerial adventures: Joseph was witnessed in flight by no less authority than Pope Urban VIII who proclaimed it a miracle. So unless you are calling the Pope a liar...

There were numerous airborne displays by Joseph— indeed his frequent and unexpected levitations so irritated his fellow monks that the good and holy men were constantly shunting him off to some other monastery.

A usually reliable dictionary of saints offered further confirmation of Joseph's aerial antics: "These [levitations] are specially remarkable in Father Joseph's case," it said, "because the evidence adduced for some of the strangest of them is of considerable weight."

And so, armed with curiosity, Douglas' book, and a willingness to drive on Italian roads starting with a spaghetti-like course down the Amalfi Coast, I resolved to go to lonely little Copertino to see the humble birthplace of St Joseph, the flying monk.

*   *   *

The Amalfi Coast wins effusive praise effortlessly: domino-like white houses and hotels stagger up sheer cliffs, small restaurants specialising in local seafood are commonplace, and the coastline is hard-edged in contrast with the smooth contours of the sea below. It is considered to be among the most spectacular drives in the world.

In towns like tiny Conca dei Marini, exotic and colourful Amalfi, and at Atrani the camera can work overtime, although it needs to be said there is already exactly the right number of garishly painted ceramic pots in the world being offered to tourists lacking taste and discernment.

We skip through unattractive Salerno and across country toward Potenza from where we will turn south east to the region of Puglia and down to the small town of Copertino.

The route takes us across the back of the Monti Picentini region and the car pulls hard against the steady incline. We are in high farmland with few other vehicles to ignore, and even fewer small towns. It is a curious thing but the towns—more correctly villages on mountain tops—always appear larger in distance. The sheer-sided rocks on which they are built take on the appearance of houses. But when you get there, there is often no "there" there.

We have left behind the region of Campania and are now in Basilicata, one of the least romantic parts of Italy. Some 25 years ago while studying Italian, I was introduced to the notion of the Mezzogiorno.

The conflated word translates literally to midday— "mezzo" meaning middle and "giorno", day—and it is the time of heat and stupor. But when applied to the southern regions of Basilicata, Campagna, Puglia and Calabria it can be pejorative, the place of laziness.

We can feel the incessant energy of Naples and the calm beauties of Sorrento being shaved away with each passing town as we drive towards Potenza on empty back roads through impressive mountains. There's not that much to look forward to however.

"The best way to see Potenza is quickly and by night," says a guide book. "That way you'll avoid the sight of some of the most brutal housing blocks you are ever likely to see."

It would be pleasing to report this is not only uncharitable but also unfair, however on arrival at this city we put away the camera for fear the lens might shatter. Potenza is a loop of motorway junctions in a valley with the town itself rising steeply up a sharp cliff. We drive to the top to find a hotel with a commanding view of hazy mountains, rooftops and the brutally ugly housing blocks.

That night, because there are no small trattoria within walking distance—and everything is severely up-hill on the way back—we go to the bar in the Grand Hotel Potenza before dinner. I have a glass of the excellent local red, Rio Nero, on the recommendation of the barman, but everything after that disappoints.

In the large and deserted dining room a couple of kids—the chef's at a guess—watch a typically loud and garishly lit television game show where the hostess looks like a transvestite wearing someone else's eyelashes.

The competing teams include an alarming number of bleached blond women with breast implants and sleazy-looking older—if not elderly—men.

One admirable feature of Italian television is it is not afraid to feature intelligent and articulate people talking direct to camera for long periods of time. On the other hand there are shows like this ridiculously protracted advertisement for silicon where no one has anything to say—intelligent or otherwise—for equally long periods of time.

I pick up the newspaper. There is, as always, some new Berlusconi scandal.

Dinner arrives and it is average at best.

Among the many myths about Italy—and the most pre-eminent if you believe television celebrity chefs who tour this country with relentless and heavily sponsored enthusiasm—is that the food is always excellent.

I too have had superb meals in towns, cities and people's homes. But as I poke listlessly at the tasteless veal before me I recall the lunch in Venice a week ago with my father-in-law.

We were at a small, family-run trattoria in the old Jewish ghetto area, some way from the tourist trail, and it wasn't high season. We wanted little more than a bottle of wine (which proved very good) and a plate of something to talk over. My spaghetti pescatora came with barely warmed chunks of surimi.

Italians can do lousy food as well as anyone.

Norman Douglas—considering the myths about Italy, especially a country which even today still has a baffling and protracted legal system wrote: "How seriously we take this nation! Almost as seriously as we take ourselves. The reason is that most of us come to Italy too undiscerning, too reverent; in the pre-critical and pre-humorous stages. We arrive here stuffed with Renaissance ideals or classical lore, and view the present through coloured spectacles."

* * *

Douglas was a rare man: he possessed a sharp, insightful wit and keen critical faculties; spoke five languages and read both Latin and Greek; was adventurous, tough and resourceful; became renown as an unashamed hedonist; and played more than passable piano.

He also had a penchant for young boys.

Born in 1868 in Austria, Douglas—whose family were Scottish—spent much of his early life in various British and European schools (all of which he hated) and developed what he called a "healthy contempt for all education", as the gifted often have the luxury of doing.

He loved natural history and at 20 visited Naples and Sorrento where he would spend much of his later life in a kind of elegant, self-indulgent exile. He would celebrate the region as "Siren Land," a reference to the women in Greek myth who lured sailors to their deaths in this area.

He lived in London for much of his young manhood, initially writing on natural history, and then joined the diplomatic service. At 26 he was posted to St. Petersburg but two years later was obliged to leave the service quickly—and the city of St Petersburg—as the result of an indiscreet love affair with a woman whispered to have been a member of the Imperial family.

He settled in Naples where he bought and renovated

a villa in the cool Posilippo area, and married his cousin Elizabeth FitzGibbon in 1898, with whom he had two sons.

He wrote stories and pamphlets about the Isle of Capri where he moved after his divorce in 1904. In 1915 he published his most successful travel book, the freewheeling and surprisingly modern *Old Calabria*, the text I am travelling to Copertino with.

Yet there is more to Douglas than that of erudite travel writer, and author of the once very popular novel *South Wind*.

In 1916 he wrote *London Games*, a book about children's games based on close observation—and, not so coincidentally, he was arrested for sexual misconduct with a young boy.

As Jonathan Keates observes in the introduction to the 1994 edition of *Old Calabria*, "after a crucial encounter in a Neapolitan street some years previously, Douglas had renounced heterosexuality for the kind of pederasty which transformed curly headed street urchins and unwashed ragamuffins on the beach into Hellenic ephebes [beautiful young men chosen for special instruction] and Ganymedes."

Keates adds it doesn't take any great alertness to note the number of times in *Old Calabria* that Douglas engages young boys.

Not that he probably needed to. His companion—never mentioned in the book—was a 12-year old English boy called Eric Wolton whom he had picked up in London.

Eric,   unfortunately,   wrote   no   book   of   his

impressions.

*   *   *

Less dramatically, I am travelling with Megan and she charts the course after unlovely Potenza down through Basilicata toward the coastal city of Taranto. The drive is relentlessly unappealing, and such small towns as I thought I might find to poke around in— to drink cheap regional wine with locals and generally enjoy for their own sake—are either non-existent or shabby and unwelcoming.

This adventure to Copertino was intended to take in quaint southern villages—but it is increasingly apparent it isn't going to offer up much other than rock, scrappy land and amaro, the bitter liqueur which is the speciality of the region.

As Douglas observed, I have come here viewing the present through coloured spectacles. How seriously we take this nation, how seriously we take ourselves.

We stop at some two-street, three-car village and in the bar at noon I greet the owner. He puts down our beers and turns away without a word. As do a number of others in the street where I amble hopefully, but briefly.

The local soccer team is getting off a swish bus. An away-game obviously. I ask, how did you do...

Nothing.

I go back inside. A group of old men is playing cards in the front room of the bar but there seems no point in interrupting them. One gets up and shuts the door on me when it looks like I might be walking towards them.

Fine. No one has to engage me let alone be interested in me.

We buy some amaro in a nearby shop and make our contribution to the local economy.

We move on slowly through the Mezzogiorno.

Many of the villages and towns we stop at—hopefully looking for a conversation—are punctuated by empty houses which confirm that a substantial percentage of this population has moved to the industrialised cities further south—or north, or anywhere else—in search of work.

This is born out when we reach the port city of Taranto, the single most frightful city I have ever seen. And I have been to brutally ugly Port Arthur in Texas, the oil town Janis Joplin left the moment she could.

We press on through the blank landscape which gives us time to consider the life of St Joseph who has drawn us into this unfortunate and inhospitable region.

*   *   *

The patron saint of pilots, air travellers and astronauts we know as St Joseph of Copertino was born Giuseppe Desa in 1603.

He was ... let us say, a simple boy.

His playmates called him "bocca-aperta" for his constantly agape mouth. He was, to be blunt, dullwitted. One source refers to him as "The Dunce".

References we might expect to be flattering say he was absent-minded, that a sudden noise would alarm him, he had no conversation, was underfed and sickly, caught every disease available, and was frequently slumped on death's doorstep.

Nobody, not even his long-suffering parents according to one account, much liked him.

It is reported by Norman Douglas that when the unfortunate Giuseppe was 17 he still couldn't distinguish brown bread from white. Around that time he saw a wandering friar begging and—perhaps because he was unpopular, unwanted and incapable of holding down any other employment—thought this might be something he could feasibly do.

Realistically, his options in smalltown Copertino were somewhat limited.

However because of his unappealing nature Giuseppe was refused admittance into various convents and, on the rare occasions he was accepted, the adolescent and awkward Giuseppe proved so intolerably clumsy that the monks who had engaged him to wash dishes and do sundry menial tasks would quickly dismiss him.

He was finally accepted as a servant at a Franciscan convent in Grottella near Copertino.

He may have been illiterate but he was faithful and dedicated, and seemed always to be happy, even though the monks made him sleep with the monastery mule. Giuseppe was a simple soul, and possibly a simpleton.

Yet he possessed something—a child-like belief in the mercy of God perhaps?—which attracted village folk to him.

Although incapable of study he was ordained by curious chance: with a group of candidates he was presented to the bishop for an oral examination on the Scriptures. However after hearing the first few candidates speak so persuasively, the bishop cut short the questioning and announced they would all be ordained.

Giuseppe did not have to endure a blind-test extrapolation on a given Biblical text, and was ordained at the age of 25 along with the other candidates.

Which explains why he is also the patron saint of test takers.

Giuseppe remained modest and knew his limitations. In a parallel with St Francis, in whose order he belonged, the man who slept with the mule now referred to himself as Brother Ass.

But then began a rare transformation.

Even as a boy Giuseppe had drifted into absent-minded dream states, but these now began to take the form of wonder-filled reveries and—again, much like St Francis—he began to experience God manifest in all things.

While in such states Giuseppe was impervious to pain: irritated fellow monks would poke him with pins and burning embers to try to rouse him. Over time the intensity of his reveries allowed him to depart from the constraints of this world and levitate.

It is said that in Copertino alone he flew more than 70 times.

When in his early 40s—a good age during that period—he was transferred to Assisi and in 1645 flew before the Spanish ambassador to the Pope, his wife, and a company of others. After that it seemed to be impossible to keep the idiot boy down.

It was said at the sight of a crucifix, an image of the Virgin or a holy relic he would fly in ecstasy.

His levitations were hailed as far away as France, Germany and Poland, and he counted among his admirers Catholic cardinals and European royalty, including the Duke of Brunswick who went to Assisi specifically to witness a flight... and converted from Lutheranism on witnessing Joseph sail across the room.

Giuseppe became so well-known that towards the end of his life—during which he also drove out devils, healed the lame, caused the blind to see, and made wine and bread multiply—his superiors confined him to a convent at Osimo.

There is a story about him preaching to sheep, much as St Francis delivered his Sermon To The Birds.

He died at Osimo at age 61. Or 60, depending on who you read.

Curiously Norman Douglas, who was so taken with the life of Joseph, didn't actually visit his birthplace of Copertino.

But I was going, and not just because of Douglas' account of an airborne individual.

Years ago I had been to another place where a whole race of men flew...

*   *   *

The afternoon was oppressively humid when Dal-

vanius Prime—a huge man in a vivid pink and un-
flatteringly skin-hugging track suit—drove me to the
entrance of the Takirau Marae some 50 kilometres up
the winding Waitotara River valley.

We were in New Zealand's Taranaki Province on
the west coast of the North Island.

It was early 1988 and Dalvanius—who died of cancer in late 2002 at age 54—was taking me to see the
home of the kahui rere, the flying men.

Dalvanius—or Dal, as he was known to most New
Zealanders—was one of the country's great musicians,
a charismatic and good-humoured man, and in later
life an inspirational cultural figure.

He had grown up playing music and singing on
marae and in small halls, and in 1969 he formed the
Fascinations with some family members. They won
a talent quest and, encouraged, started touring Aus-
tralasia. Dal proved himself remarkably gifted, and an
intuitive singer, arranger and producer.

He was a big man with a huge heart, and appalling
taste in clothes and interior design. The enormous gilt-
framed image of the bust of Tutankhamun above his
bed which he showed me proudly was actually a framed
beach towel he'd bought at the British Museum gift
shop.

On this afternoon, however, we were on a journey
through his past to coincide with the release of an album by Patea Maori, the cultural group from the small
and beleaguered nearby town of Patea.

The rural town had been in emotional and financial
free-fall before Dal arrived to inspire local Maori.

The freezing works had closed and there was widespread unemployment. The recession of the late 80s and early 90s hit Patea a decade before the rest of the country. Yet Dal saw the other side of the equation: Maori had been forced to rediscover their tikanga, their history and heritage, which included the distinctive local style of carving, and music.

Dal recorded the upbeat and catchy song *Poi E* with members of the local Maori Club, added the sound of miked-up poi to give it a percussive depth, and released it to the utter indifference of influential big city radio programmers who recoiled at a pop song sung in Maori.

It took 18 months for the song to climb the charts but in that time it became a national classic. Even now, decades later, it is hard to find someone who lived in New Zealand at that time—no matter what age— whose heart doesn't melt with sentimental affection on hearing it.

An album should have followed but it was delayed when Dal's mentor and musical partner Ngoi Pewhairangi—who had written *Poi E*—died when he and Patea Maori were touring in Europe on the back of their addictive hit.

They were fulfilling a promise he'd made her and the club members to take their music to the world. They'd even sung on the stage at the Apollo Theatre in New York which, for Dal—a soul music lover whose record label Maui Music was to be the start of what he called "a Maori Motown"—must have been like arriving at the end of the rainbow.

The *Poi E* album eventually came out three years later—it had been delayed further by the death in '86 of Dal's cousin Greg Carroll, road manger of U2 whom the band acknowledged in their song *One Tree Hill.*

When the album was released it went past most people. It didn't have another breakthrough song like *Poi E* but it was a minor masterpiece of production by Dal who worked on a thin budget.

"Everyone in the studio calls me Dalvanius De Mille," he laughed about his wide-screen sound. "My ultimate hero is Phil Spector who either made a classic or a real bomb."

Dal had made both.

But on this afternoon in the valley he had something else on his mind. The fanciful cover for the *Poi E* album, illustrated by artist and film-maker Joe Wylie, was of figures from Maori mythology.

Half-men, half-tuatara characters emerge from the water and above them flying men circle in the air.

These flying men are the kahui rere and this river valley, the apex of the traditional boundary of the Ngaa Rauru people was where they lived.

The story—Dal advised me not to say "the legend"—of the kahui rere, who originated at an island off the coast, is well documented. According to historian S. Percy Smith, writing in 1910, "a placenta was cast into the sea and in due course became a man whose name was Whanau-moana or Sea-born. He had wings, as had his descendants. At first none of these beings had stationary homes, but flew about from place to place, sometimes alighting on the tops of mountains."

The last of these people were named Te Kahui Rere and settled in the low hills of the Waitotara River valley.

Dal points to the cliffs above the marae and indicates areas which are tapu because bones of kahui rere were found.

"The kahui rere were my ancestors and as a child of Ngaa Rauru, my tribal affiliation on my mother's side, the kahui rere were our tipuna, our ancestors, and are not just mythological.

"They are part of our living being."

I look at the hills to which Dal is pointing.

Later I sit outside the hall of the marae while Dal is inside fiddling with a cheap tape recorder. The Maori here at Takirau marae, where he often came to relax away from the other world he lived in, had lost a cassette of some songs he had left for them to learn. He needs to re-record them.

A solitary fly buzzes in the thick air as his sweet voice lifts into the dense and unfamiliar humidity of the countryside around me.

The hills blaze a rich green and under a cloudless sky even my cynical city-born heart felt the timelessness and mysterious quality of this place.

In that magical moment—and I tell Megan this as we drive through southern Italy to the birthplace of the idiot boy Giuseppe—as I looked across the hilltops I truly believed that a long time ago maybe, just maybe, men could fly.

*   *   *

Giuseppe Desa was not the only aerial member of
that extensive catalogue of misfits, the tragic and de-
luded, sometimes criminally suspect, and often inspirational figures known as Catholic saints.

Agnes of Montepulciano (1268–1327) was said to
levitate while at prayer. She entered the monastery in
Montepulciano at age nine, at 13 was charged by Pope
Nicholas IV with establishing a monastery at Proceno,
and became its prioress at 15.

This precocious over-achiever then went on an aus-
terity binge: she slept on the ground with a stone for
her pillow; lived on bread and water; but it is said
flowers would bloom around her when she kneeled in
prayer.

It was told at the moment of her death that all the
babies in the region, no matter how young, began to
speak of Agnes's piety and her passing.

Then there was also the levitating Catherine of Si-
enna (1347–1380) who at age 16 assigned herself to
seclusion in her own home for three years, only leaving her room to go to Mass or Confession, lived on a
spoonful of herbs a day and slept only a few hours.

She rejoined the world and gathered followers, ex-
perienced visions of Heaven and Hell, and was battered
by the political vicissitudes of the church at this volatile
period during which she advocated peace between the
Papacy and various principalities. She wrote insightful

books on the nature of Man and spirituality, and died aged 33.

Teresa of Avila (1515–1582) wrote in her autobiography of the divine ecstatic state during which the enraptured body is possessed by the spirit and is so intoxicated that the body will fly for a period of half an hour. She is said to have been uncomfortable while in this state and tried to prevent it happening.

"But little precautions are unavailing when Our Lord will have it otherwise".

That Catholic-sounding quote comes from Paramhansa Yogananda's *Autobiography of Yogi*, published in 1950. The great mystic and teacher—who introduced Hindu spirituality to the United States at the request of his guru Sri Yukteswar—is recounting his experience of Bhaduri Mahasaya, a yogi who also, it is said, flew.

Of the habits of mystics and the divinely empowered Mahasaya told Yogananada: "Saints are not only rare but disconcerting. Even in scripture they are found embarrassing."

Mahasaya might have been talking about St Joseph of Copertino and the trouble he gave his fellow monks when he would spontaneously levitate.

*   *   *

Human history is littered with myths about men and women who flew: Lilitu was a Sumerian flying demon who attacked men in their sleep; Icarus had help from wings his father Daedalus made; the Chinese emperor Shun was taught to fly by two women in his court; Perseus borrowed the winged shoes of Mercury; Hermes was the messenger of the Greek gods; Nike the daughter of Pallas and Styx whose image appears on Summer Olympics medals; Sally Field as *The Flying Nun*; Superman...

Flying men are found in folklore from Uganda—the king Nakivingi using an invisible flying warrior Kibaga to hurl rocks down on his enemies—and Egypt, to the aboriginal tribes of Australia, and the rich stories of Native Americans.

Black Elk had a vision of flying men when he was five, and Mojave tribes worshipped Mastamho, a warrior who transformed himself into an eagle.

The stories of Man entering a dream state and flying as a bird are legion.

And we wouldn't want to start counting the many ways in which Man flew: on winged horses, flying carpets; the Russian hag Baba Yaga who flew around in a mortar...

Flight has preoccupied Mankind since we first looked at birds and leaves blowing in the wind.

And Man has celebrated this in song: images of flight, soaring, wings and so forth litter popular and High Art songs through all cultures.

But if we suspend disbelief and surrender to the collective dream-memory of Man, why should a man not fly?

And if so, why not in the small town of Copertino?

*   *   *

The torpid town is dozing in the midmorning heat of a late summer day when we arrive. We circle the massive Castello Angioni and I park near a great arch topped by a statue of a beatific St Joseph, his outstretched arms reaching Heavenward.

Down a narrow lane opposite, between shuttered houses is the Santuario S Giuseppe da Copertino, the church built in his honour and on the site of his modest birthplace.

An old woman sees us coming, rude intruders, and scuttles back inside.

The whitewashed houses are silent, a dog trots in the narrow streets.

Giuseppe Desa, St Joseph, came from a family that was reasonably wealthy. His altruistic father, Felice Desa—a carpenter it is said—got into debt through signing promissory notes to help some friends. The friends disappeared and he had to answer for the debts. The authorities went looking for him and, to avoid jail, he hid in nearby scrub.

This seemingly pointless anecdote, probably apocryphal, sets the scene for what happened later.

When his wife, Francesca, was about to give birth to Giuseppe, the bailiffs arrived for her husband yet again and she sought refuge in the stable across the lane.

And so Giuseppe—Saint Joseph—was born in a stable.

Norman Douglas doubts this story and suggests it might have been a convenient, later fabrication since Giuseppe became a Franciscan and that is a branch of the Christian faith which embraces the humble.

The Franciscans were not above recreating their saints in imitation of Christ, St Francis himself—despite coming from a well-to-do family—just happened to be born in a stable as well, La Stalletta near the main piazza in Assisi.

The chapel on the site has become a place where locals pray for the needs of their children, and where expectant mothers go to pray for a healthy pregnancy.

In his book *In the Footsteps of Francis and Clare*, the writer Roch Niemer who takes tour groups around Franciscan holy sites—acknowledges this story of St Francis is known only through legend, no documents exist to prove it.

He cites an old translation which says, "... a stranger came to the threshold of the blessed house [of Francis's mother Pica who was having trouble giving birth] and gave the young wife the mysterious message that she would not be able to give birth to her baby except in a stable, in the same way that Mary bore Jesus. So Pica was taken to the stable next to the family house. There, on the straw, the baby who would become St Francis first saw the light of day."

This legend, says Niemer, is "the gentle starting point" for Francis's conformity to Christ.

So too, the legend that Giuseppe was born in similar Christ-like circumstances—and that both had father's who were carpenters simply added to Giuseppe's cachet.

Whatever the truth, a church was built to enclose the stable in Copertino which now contains the relic of Giuseppe's heart.

It is a moving, ill-lit shrine with that relic on one wall and the suggestions of stable décor scattered around. Sort of a Disneyworld verisimilitude of a stable.

But on the walls of the church are two paintings, one on each side of the bright altar, both depicting St Joseph in flight.

Inside this empty church, despite the soaring height and the gleaming altar, it feels gloomy and...

I squint into the paintings and the altarpiece, searching for meaning.

Later in the afternoon a few old men and a middle-aged woman come in to offer prayers and the priest holds confession.

There is a sense of the little-changing ages here.

The old people stare briefly, but with unnerving intensity, then shuffle off. Even though I am sitting in respectful silence I am made to feel like the rude intruder that undoubtedly I am.

It is humid and a solitary fly buzzes noisily in the thick air.

Outside I walk towards the middle-aged priest in black robes who pointedly turns away, then disappears through a small wooden door beside the chapel.

I stand outside the church and birthplace of Saint Joseph and try to conjure up what this place must have looked like all those centuries ago: the stable; the idiot boy playing in the dirty streets being ignored by the other children of the village; his long-suffering parents making a bolt for it when they saw him coming towards them...

It has been a long journey and an even more strange pilgrimage for me, not even a lapsed Catholic, to have made. I stand here at the birthplace of this flying saint and feel... well, not a lot actually.

Rain spits down and Megan steps in some gritty and gummy dogshit outside the saint's house.

Oh, fuckit. Saints? Who needs 'em?

*　　*　　*

Most people—especially those not of a faith which believes in them—have become immune to the existence of saints. We have heard about so damn many of them. Especially in the last quarter of the 20th century when saints were arriving faster than boy bands and controversial Madonna videos.

The late Pope John Paul II, history's most frequent-flyer pope, rarely kissed the tarmac of a new country without first beatifying or canonising some local contenders for sainthood. The man was profligate when it came to opening the gates of heaven to the most hallowed.

As a Vatican source once observed on the induction of a new batch of these holies-in-a-hurry: "From Papua New Guinea to Paraguay, Australia to Africa, he wants to give every colour, every country, every culture a saint to believe in."

John Paul II was referred to as "the saint-maker" because of his propensity to create saints, and more than just occasionally he was elevating some into the white-robed pantheon whose history was unknown or faith suspect.

John Paul II created more new saints than all popes in the previous four centuries combined. And you can add to that more than 1300 in the transit lounge awaiting sainthood through beatification.

Sainthood became a growth industry under his papacy and, as in the case of the Martyrs of Vietnam—100 declared saints in 1998—he was sometimes a volume dealer.

Four years earlier he'd made saints of 103 priests, missionaries and lay people who died in the early days of the Church in Korea. In late 2000 he canonised another 120 martyrs in China, many of them murdered in the Boxer Rebellion or under the Communist regime. Saints made to order.

Around half of all new saints under John Paul II came from Asia and were either local converts or missionaries. However given the paucity of information about many, questions have been raised about just how "holy" some of these people were.

Not much is known about the short life of the Vietnamese man now named John Dat, for example.

He was born in West Tonkin in 1764, ordained as a Catholic priest in 1798 then immediately arrested in one of the periodic anti-Catholic purges which punctuate Vietnam's recent history. After three months imprisonment he was beheaded for refusing to deny his faith. Johnny, we hardly knew you...

In 1900 he was beatified by Pope Leo XIII, then in 1988 was canonised by Pope John Paul II, joining that hit list of the 100 Martyrs of Vietnam.

What is of interest to those outside the Catholic Church—a question which seems not to trouble the faithful—is why John Paul II embarked on what John Allen, columnist for the *National Catholic Reporter* called "halo inflation".

"His zeal for saint-making," said Vatican specialist Orazio La Rocca, a role not dissimilar to a "Royal watcher" in Britain, "ultimately conveys a simple message to the faithful: Anyone can aspire to holiness, from the simplest priest who prays daily, to the mother who dies because she refuses an abortion, along with this century's many martyrs."

In short, he was responding to the needs of his broad constituency by allowing for local models of holiness in an increasingly secular world.

Secular writers have condescendingly referred to El Pele—Cerefino Jiminez Malla, shot by firing squad in 1936 during the Spanish Civil War for publicly defending a priest, and beatified in 1997—as "an illiterate horse trader". But that doesn't trouble the similarly illiterate faithful who identify with his deeds and faith.

This need is also evident among more sophisticated peoples. As Franco Ferrerotta, a sociologist at Rome University observed, "In an increasingly consumer-influenced society there is a need for a role model, some sign of where to go. People have always thought things could only get better in an ever-richer society. But now most people are well off, they notice the same problems still exist. It has created a deep-rooted sense of ill-being."

So what is true is, despite secular cynicism, many people still feel the need to have heroic models, whether they be Diana Princess of Wales or football-flicker David Beckham.

Such people embody attributes many aspire to. So it is with saints.

In that light Giuseppe Desa, a simpleton from a small town in impoverished 17th century Italy, had all the makings of an inspirational figure for the faithful, peasant constituency.

A century ago Norman Douglas identified this need for saints and the Church's local agents had a willingness to supply them. Less a cynic than an observer, he noted in *Old Calabria*, "From this rank soil there sprang up an exotic efflorescence of holiness. If south Italy swarmed with sinners... it also swarmed with saints."

He then considers the nature of the many saints in the south and says one cannot help but note the great uniformity of their lives, "a kind of family resemblance".

"These saints are alike—monotonously alike if you care to say so—in their chastity and other official virtues... Nearly all of them could fly, more or less; nearly all of them could cure diseases and cause the clouds to rain; nearly all were illiterate; and every one of them died in the odour of sanctity—with roseate complexion, sweet smelling corpse and flexible limbs.

"Yet each one has his particular gifts, his strong point. Joseph of Copertino specialised in flying; others were conspicuous for their heroism in sitting in hot baths, devouring ordure, tormenting themselves with pins, and so forth."

Douglas argues this diversity of gifts is because of the furious competition between the various monastic orders of the time which lead to never-ending litigation and complaints to headquarters in Rome.

"Every one of these saints, from the first drawing of his divine talents, was surrounded by an atmosphere of jealous hatred on the part of his co-religionists. If one order came out with a flying wonder, another, in frantic emulation, would introduce some new speciality to eclipse his fame—something in the fasting line, it may be; or a female mystic whose palpitating letters to Jesus Christ would melt all readers to pity."

So Giuseppe Desa—"bocca aperta"—and soon to become St Joseph of Copertino?

He served a political purpose for his order and was someone from the ranks of the great illiterate in the villages and remote hillside towns of the peninsula's impoverished Mezzogiorno. His miraculous life gave hope to those who believed a benign God could intervene in their lives and protect them.

St Joseph's elevation illustrated that all Mankind—however simple, open-mouthed and unpopular—possessed the potential for holiness.

The reports of his levitations may have been driven

by the powerful symbolism inherent in the act—
ascending heavenward—and encouraged by those in
whose best political interest it was to have an idiot
boy a saint.

That would explain his elevation into the realms of
the most holy.

He may, of course, also have flown.

*   *   *

We live in a world lacking of wonder, where ecstasy
is to be mistrusted and the faith of simple souls invites derision. In the 16th century the adjective "naïve"
meant original and natural, by extension an endearing
simplicity. And today?

A once healthy scepticism has hardened into an effortless and often reflexive cynicism which allows us to
refute without question the possibility of divine ecstasy.

Much of this has been brought on by those who
advocate the supremacy of reason.

The writer Felipe Fernandez-Armesto in his book
Truth discusses reason in a chapter which opens with
a quotation by G. K. Chesterton: "Reason itself is a
matter of faith. It is an act of faith to assert that our
thoughts have any relation to reality".

This is a time bereft of miracles, but it might be
pleasant occasionally to be open once more to the im-
possibility of them.

The American essayist and philosopher Ralph
Waldo Emerson said, "If we meet no gods it is because
we harbour none".

However he also said, "I hate quotations. Tell me what you know."

So...

*   *   *

We leave suspicious little Copertino and drive to Lecce—the home of alarmingly over-powering baroque architecture and, as it transpires, a hideously green motel room with an unimpeded view of a parking lot for longhaul trucks.

On the way through the city, however, we get caught in a downpour at dusk, and a Saturday night traffic jam. For an hour we drive around lost and confused, me increasingly angry with dead-end streets, roadworks around the chiesa, and the sullen southern people who refuse to understand my attempts at whatever Italian I can muster when I ask for directions.

As we drive down a long piece of poorly illuminated and rain-wracked road we have seen twice previously I am cursing myself: what had seemed a promising trip in search of a saint—and maybe some kind of insight into something unspecified and nameless—has actually been an utter waste of time.

There was no great epiphany, in all likelihood there was never going to be.

But maybe this journey through the beautiful then bloody awful barren landscapes, engaging with the unusual and disparate lives of Norman Douglas and the idiot boy who flew, and the memory of that rare time with Dalvanius and the spirit of the kahui rere, have been their own rewards?

Maybe.

As insipid green light from streetlamps sparkles on the windscreen; I try again to understand the world of Giuseppe Desa the flying saint, and of popes and miracles.

I wait for a sudden, deserved, insight in the night— but nothing comes. That world of faith and flying men seems so very far away.

As we are halted by carabinieri who step out of the blackness I am thinking, a flying man? Jesusgod, I wish.

White gloves in the night wave us on into more crosstown traffic and I concentrate on the rain-lashed road ahead.

And where is St Joseph of Copertino, the idiot boy born Giuseppe Desa, in all this?

Nowhere.

I find instead I am thinking of the other Giuseppe, the bushy-browed one back in Sorrento. The one who was as indifferent as this rain and the people we have encountered on this seemingly annoying and pointless—but odd, and in some ways, curiously-rewarding—journey.

Maybe all along it was he who offered the lesson I have been looking for as I have travelled.

So I will just carry on and ignore everything that is all around me.

And do it for myself.

About Public Address

Public Address is a community of New Zealand-centric writers who provide essays, analysis, commentary, reviews, and satire in an online format.

The Public Address website includes:
Russell Brown's *Hard News*
Damian Christie's *Cracker*
Graeme Edgeler's *Legal Beagle*
Jolisa Gracewood's *Busytown*
Hadyn Green's *Field Theory*
Emma Hart's *Up Front*
David Haywood's *Southerly*
Keith Ng's *OnPoint*
Fiona Rae's *Radiation*
Graham Reid's *Random Play*
David Slack's *Island Life*
and regular guest contributors.

Public Address can be found at:
www.publicaddress.net